Frederick P. Frankville, 1950

Fred and Sherry, 2012

Running with the Dogs

War in Korea with D/2/7 USMC

Frederick P. Frankville

iUniverse, Inc.
Bloomington

RUNNING WITH THE DOGS
WAR IN KOREA WITH D/2/7 USMC

iUniverse books may be ordered through booksellers or by contacting:

iUniverse
1663 Liberty Drive
Bloomington, IN 47403
www.iuniverse.com
1-800-Authors (1-800-288-4677)

ISBN: 978-1-4759-7474-4 (sc)
ISBN: 978-1-4759-8732-4 (hc)
ISBN: 978-1-4759-7475-1 (e)

Library of Congress Control Number: 2013904771

Printed in the United States of America

iUniverse rev. date: 5/29/2013

Dedication

To the marines with whom I served in Korea, and to those with whom I didn't—especially those who gave their lives so the people whose freedom they fought for could build a nation of their own.

"Hundreds of firefights, patrols, and battles take place in a war. Most are just fading memories in the minds of the survivors. Those killed are registered in the casualty reports. This also will fade to the backwaters of history and, over time, to those who are remembered on Memorial Day as the 'war dead.' The personal sacrifices and pain will be just ... dust in the wind."

Fred Frankville

Table of Contents

Foreword

An exhibit at the National Museum of the Marine Corps in Triangle, Virginia, depicts the brutal conditions that US Marines and their American, South Korean, and United Nations counterparts endured during the Korean War. It includes wary marines and US Navy corpsmen clad in winter gear in a mountain setting at night, no doubt awaiting a skirmish with enemy forces. To make the scene more realistic, museum personnel keep the temperatures in the room that houses the exhibit at a cool level.

As I was standing in front of the exhibit, I overheard a conversation between a father and his son regarding the scene. The youngster asked his dad, "Why is it so cold in here?"

"Maybe it's because the room is so big," he answered.

"Could it have anything to do with the scene?" the boy asked.

"Maybe," the dad said. "I don't know why it would, though."

The boy thought about that for a minute.

"When was the Korean War, anyway?" he wanted to know.

"I'm not sure," the dad admitted.

"Well, who was involved? And why were they fighting?"

The boy was persistent with his questions, as young children often are.

"I don't recall," the dad replied. "Let's get out of here. It's cold."

He took his son by the hand, and they left for warmer exhibits.

The conversation reminded me of people's general lack of knowledge of the Korean War, its time frame, who participated, why they fought, and why it is known as the "Forgotten War." Fred Frankville could have answered that young boy's questions. After all, he fought in Korea, saw many of his friends get wounded or die in combat, and lived to tell about it.

Unlike the boy and his father, he could not leave the "room" because it was cold. He had to endure the frigid temperatures, which sometimes dropped into the minus thirty- to fifty-degree range, the snow, the lack of hot (and sometimes cold) food, inadequate equipment, poor—often nonexistent—sanitary facilities ... in short, the assets of modern society that are often lacking completely for troops engaged in a war. Sure, he, like most of his counterparts, complained. That's what marines do best. But he had a job to do, and he did it.

As the contents of this book demonstrate, Fred Frankville was proud of what he did, despite the conditions in which he fought, the heartache he experienced due to the loss of some of his friends, the devastation he witnessed due to the constant fighting over the Korean countryside, and the overall consequences of war. After all, he contributed in part to the building of a nation that could not have grown into one of the world's top ten economies if the United Nations had not engaged the Communists hell-bent on swallowing up the southern part of Korea and folding it into a unified Communist nation.

Here is a brief—very brief—and greatly simplified history of how the Korean War began. Japan ruled Korea between 1905 and the end of World War II. After the war ended, Russia and the United States divided the country into two sections separated by the 38th parallel. On June 25, 1950, North Korea, backed by Russia and China, invaded a woefully unprepared South Korea in an attempt to annex it. The United Nations came to the aid of South Korea.

The North Koreans were successful in the early days of the invasion. The United Nations committed troops, mostly Americans, to drive the North Koreans back. In all, twenty-two countries (including South Korea) contributed ground troops, air force units, naval elements, hospital personnel, and other modes of support to the UN effort. By mid-September 1950 they turned the tide and drove the North Koreans back. Then, in October 1950, the Chinese entered the war.

The two sides fought up and down the Korean peninsula for the next two and a half years, with neither side gaining a decided advantage. Eventually, they signed a treaty ending the fighting on July 27, 1953. Technically, they are still at war—sixty years later. And there it rests.

Note: The history of the Korean War cannot be summed up in three paragraphs. The account presented above is a thumbnail sketch that makes no attempt to describe the complexities or nuances involved in the events leading up to, involved in, or ending the fighting. Readers are invited to pursue their own studies to get a fuller picture of the politics of the war.

In all, the fighting lasted for thirty-eight months. Fred

Frankville's part included almost thirteen months (which seemed like a lifetime to him), from December 6, 1950, to November, 28, 1951. He was in Dog Co. nine months and S2 intelligence for six weeks. For the rest of his time in Korea he was a member of a 4.2 mortar company until his tour ended. In this book, he describes one marine's part, which is a far cry from an overall picture of the war. But he gives readers a clear idea of what the war was like for one marine and his Korean War experience. That is what he set out to do when he began *Running with the Dogs*. He certainly does not leave readers cold with his story.

Arthur G. Sharp

Arthur G. Sharp is the editor of *Korea Veterans: The Graybeards*, the bimonthly eighty-page magazine published by the Korean War Veterans Association. He served in the Marine Corps from 1958 to 1962.

Acknowledgments

I thank the many people who have contributed to the contents of this book by adding their own remembrances, reading the manuscript before it went to print, and helping with the myriad tasks that go into preparing a book. Fighting a war is not a one-person operation; neither is writing a book. I didn't fight the war alone, as the contents of this book suggest. And I didn't write the book by myself. It's a product of teamwork—and I am grateful for everyone who contributed to the book's creation.

Special thanks go to Art Sharp, a fellow marine, who edited this manuscript and offered valuable suggestions regarding the publishing process. People often joke that it is hard to find a marine who can read or write. But we managed to combine our reading and writing skills to produce this book. There is hope yet for marines.

Semper Fi to all of them who have served in the past, are serving in the present, or who will serve in the future.

Chapter 1
Why I Never Went to Parris Island

One Happy "Dog"

I was not born a US Marine. Nobody is. Marines are made, not born. As the US Marine Corps recruiting posters proclaim, the title of marine is "Earned, Not Given." When I was a kid, I did not harbor any ambitions to either earn or receive the title. But events have a funny way of altering the directions of people's lives. They certainly did for me. That is why I became a member of Dog Company, Seventh Marine Regiment, First Marine Division (D/7) from December 6, 1950, to September 1951 as a rifleman, then fire-team leader, and eventually squad leader.

Later, I was in S2 (intelligence), attached to Easy Company and Dog Company for six weeks. Following that, I was transferred to a 4.2 mortar company until my departure from Korea on December 3, 1951.

I was—and still am—proud to be a member of "Dog" Company and the US Marine Corps. I am prouder still of my service in Korea. It was not always a pleasant time. In fact, it was downright gruesome on occasion. Nevertheless, it was rewarding. My time in the Marine Corps was one of those life-changing events that pushed me in a different direction, and I am happy that I did not resist the change.

From Naples to Rock Island

I am a first-generation American—one of five children born to Italian immigrants. My father left Naples, Italy, in 1905 at fifteen years of age and went to New York, where he moved in with a relative for a year or so. From New York he went to Milwaukee and then to Rock Island, Illinois, where he met my mother. She was born in Prizzi, Italy, and came to America in 1912. They must have wondered if they had gotten sidetracked in Belgium by mistake.

Belgian Neighborhood

The ethnic makeup of my neighborhood was mostly Belgian. A Belgian consulate was in the next town over. My schoolmates and playground friends were mostly first-generation Belgian Americans. Belgian, Italian—it didn't make much difference in Rock Island.

The city was a safe place in which to grow up. We were next to the Mississippi River and went swimming and fishing a lot. We were about five blocks from a city refuse center, so we knew what trucks to follow to get a lot of good stuff. That led to a lot of fun at times.

A Moving Experience

One day a pharmaceutical truck showed up, and the driver threw out a lot of old drugs, including several cases of Ex-Lax. We peeled off the labels and filled our pockets.

Along came our friend "Peanuts" Knoefrl. He walked and

ran like he was climbing steps. He asked, "What did you find?"

We said, "Hershey bars."

He asked for some, so we filled his pockets, and Peanuts started eating the stuff with both hands. We were all walking toward the park several blocks away when Peanuts said that he had to go to the bathroom. He started to run toward home, then he hesitated for a moment, and then he just kept on running.

Peanuts did not go to school for several days. When we saw him later, he looked like a whooping crane. He told us that he had been in the hospital and the doctor had told him that the Hershey bars were Ex-Lax. We pleaded innocent.

Peanuts joined the Marine Corps after high school. One hot day in Korea, our company was walking alongside a road across from the Fifth Marines. There was a guy walking toward us from the opposite side of the road who walked like he was climbing stairs. I thought that it just had to be Peanuts—and it was.

We met in the center of the road and hugged each other. I asked him if he would like a Hershey bar, and he said, "Hell, no!"

Peanuts stayed in the marines after the Korean War and was killed in Vietnam at DaNang.

St. Joseph School: The Parris Island of Rock Island

I went to St. Joseph School in Rock Island from first to eighth grade. This school was run by nuns who believed in quality education under strict discipline. They came from a religious order founded in Ireland in 1830. They had BVM behind their names. This was an abbreviation of "Blessed Virgin Mary."

The nuns were meaner than the proverbial junkyard dogs.

Believe me, Parris Island boot camp would have been a breeze for anyone who attended St. Joseph. Those nuns could teach the meanest drill instructors (DIs) a few tricks about creative bullying. (Come to think of it, maybe that's why the Marine Corps never sent me to Parris Island or San Diego for boot camp. They knew I had attended St. Joseph, so there was nothing the DIs could teach me.)

The nuns had fifty students to a class, but the boys and girls were so well disciplined you could hear a pin drop in a classroom. We were all too scared to do anything that would upset the teacher.

The boys sat in one section of the classroom and the girls in another. If a boy spoke to the girl across the aisle from him and the nun caught him, she made him carry a big ugly rag doll all day. If she caught one of the boys doing this for the second time, she not only made him carry the doll, but she let him out of class several minutes early and ordered him to stand outside the building in front of the exit doors, doll in hand, as six hundred students walked by him. This made the boys hate the girls—and dolls.

If a girl was caught talking to a boy during class, both the girl and the boy had to go up to the head of the class (which was about the only way I could ever get there). They had to put their hands out, palm up, and the nun would smack both with a ruler. It was easier to carry the doll.

After the fourth grade the girls had to wear uniforms that all looked alike. The boys all had to wear ties. If by chance one of the boys forgot to wear a tie, the nuns had a replacement tie that they would pin on him. It was a huge red bowtie made out of crepe paper, and it stuck out past the shoulders. Boys who forgot their tie had to wear this for the rest of the day.

I don't know of a boy who had to wear this more than

once. The first thing that I put on when I was getting dressed for school was my tie.

When the nun asked us what we wanted to be when we were adults, most of the boys said they wanted to be policemen or pilots or firemen. I said I wanted to be a priest. I thought if I told them that, they would be gentle with me when they hit me with their ruler. I don't think it worked. At any rate, I never became a priest, and they didn't hit me any more gently.

Even Marine Recruits Had It Easier Than This

We went home every day with an armload of books. We had about three hours' worth of homework. While the kids in public school were having fun and enjoying life after the school day was over, those of us from St. Joseph were locked in our houses doing homework. It was very depressing.

During midmorning at school we had a restroom break. We all walked down the stairs and stood at attention, one pupil on each step. The girls were on the other side of the stairway, and a wall was in the center of the stairs. The nun positioned herself to watch both sides of the steps.

First we took a drink of water. Then one student at a time went to the restroom. When the student in the restroom was done, he went back up the stairs. Then the next student got a drink of water and went to the restroom. This was repeated until the last student had a drink and had gone to the restroom.

I was never in the restroom with another student. We also did not get a second drink of water. If we did, we would get hit with the ruler.

In 1943, the boys and girls had a math contest on the blackboard. When one or the other was done with the problem, they went to their desks in a military manner. The students did not go directly to their desks. They had to go to the end of the room, turn left to the next wall, and then turn left and go up the aisle to their desk—never walking in front of anyone.

There was a pretty girl named Rita, who looked like Shirley Temple. I had kind of a hankering for her, although she didn't know it. One day she walked behind me, and for some insane reason I stuck my foot out. She tripped over it and fell flat on her face.

The nun, who was in the back of the room sitting on a stool with a ruler, came racing up the aisle toward me. I gritted my teeth, waiting to get the hell beat out of me. Instead, she beat the kid next to me into the ground like a tent peg. I think he thought he had made a mistake on the blackboard. I was petrified. I wanted to say, "Stop. I did it," but I was too scared. For several weeks this bothered me.

Maybe It's Not a Good Thing to Admit to a Bad Thing

On graduation day from eighth grade we had a ceremony. Monsignor Durkin gave a little speech telling us we were the leaders of tomorrow and to go to Mass and obey our parents. After this little speech we were given a stale doughnut and a weak cup of cocoa. The reward emboldened me.

I was still bothered about the fact that someone else took a beating for tripping Rita when I was to blame. So, as a matter of conscience, I went up to the nun who did the beating. Her name was Sister Mary Judette. She was lanky and had bright red eyebrows.

I said, "Sister Mary Judette, remember when you beat Richard up for tripping Rita?"

She said, "What about it?"

"Richard did not trip Rita," I admitted.

"Who did?" she asked.

"I did."

She screamed, "You did!"—and she sucker punched me in the teeth.

"You let someone else take the blame?" Sister Mary Judette roared, and proclaimed that I was going to reform school.

Well, I wasn't going to let that intimidate me, since it seemed like a better choice.

"I am in reform school," I retorted.

I do believe that if the room had not been crowded with people, she would have taken another punch at me. I went to ninth grade at a public school. *Free at last!*

In all fairness to the nuns, they did give us a quality education and a sense of values that endures to this day. We were taught to speak coherently and factually, and to be prepared to prove what we say before we say it. Now people make throwaway statements, and they say, "Prove me wrong." This is the opposite of the way the nuns taught us. The nuns also taught us academics far beyond our grade levels.

I know college graduates who would not have graduated from eighth grade at St. Joseph School. I would like to reach back in time, borrow Sister Mary Judette's ruler, and slap some of these laggards alongside of the head.

St. Joseph School has been demolished now. The new Rock Island County Jail is on the site. If the nuns were in charge of the county jail, I know there would not be any repeat offenders there.

Chapter 2
Let the Earning Process Begin

Three Sons Serve

I was one of three sons; all three of us served in the military. In 1940 one of my older brothers went into the army and eventually rose to the rank of lieutenant colonel. After he retired from the army, he went into teaching and received a doctorate degree in history. My oldest brother joined the navy in 1942.

My path to the military was a bit different. I became a member of the Twenty-First Engineer Battalion when I joined the Marine Reserve in May 1950 in Moline, Illinois. The USMCR center was located on River Drive in Moline, where I ended up when a friend of mine asked me if I would like to join the Marine Corps Reserve with him.

"Okay," I said. "It sounds interesting."

He said, "I will meet you there at the next meeting night."

That was the recruiting process. I found out later that his

brother was doing some recruiting for the reserve center in Moline.

I went to the reserve center and signed up. My friend never got there. When I called him later, he said he would make the next meeting. He didn't show up for that one either. He joined the Naval Reserve.

War Breaks Out

The Korean War started on June 25, 1950, when Communist North Korea invaded South Korea. The United Nations intervened and asked member nations to send troops. Naturally, the United States responded, even though it was a bit short of troops at the time.

Like the rest of the military, the Marine Corps was undermanned and desperate to have boots on the ground as quickly as possible in Korea. Reservists activated in the early days of the war in August 1950 were sent directly to Camp Pendleton, California, trading basic training for rudimentary field drills. They joined the ranks of the World War II veterans sent to Korea.

My records show that on August 17, 1950, our unit—the Twenty-First Engineer Company—was transferred into Casual Company, Headquarters Battalion, Training & Replacement Command. The next day we all boarded a train at Rock Island, Illinois, for Camp Pendleton, California. I didn't know what was in store for me, but I was ready for almost anything, thanks to my pre-boot-camp training by the nuns at St Joseph School.

Train Trip to California

Camp Pendleton was one of the largest marine bases in the world. The base was almost empty when we arrived. It had a fire brigade and little else. Pendleton had hundreds of barracks and other buildings, all with boarded-up windows. The water was turned off, and five years of dust was over everything. We had to turn on the water, knock the boards off the windows, wash them, scrub the decks, and light all the water heaters in all the vacant buildings.

Armed guards were at the mess hall to keep reservists out. There were no provisions to feed the thousands of reservists who arrived daily. Field stoves and picnic tables were set up to serve chow. For breakfast, we got two pancakes, one orange, and coffee.

For lunch, we bought bread and lunch meat at the PX (post exchange). We shared with those who did not have money to buy their own lunch. For supper, we got two baloney sandwiches, one apple, and coffee.

I made a phone call to my brother in San Diego and asked to borrow five dollars so I could purchase food. More mess halls were opened later.

We could not leave the base until we got assigned to a unit. One day the folks in charge called us out on a parade ground. An officer with a bullhorn asked for those with former military service to "stand as you are." (I stood fast.)

He said, "Those who did not go to boot camp in any service fall out to the right."

Those who had previous service went to Tent Camp 2. The camp actually had Quonset huts, not tents. The Corps issued M-1 rifles to us, and we spent a day or so taking the M-1 apart. We had to do it blindfolded. We then spent several days shooting the rifle at stationary and moving targets. It was a fun time, but it hardly prepared us for combat. The fun ended abruptly.

"Cruising" on the Collins

Around November 15, 1950, we, the third replacement draft, boarded the USS *General E. T. Collins* (AP 147) at San Diego, California. There were about seventeen hundred of us. I thought it was an ugly ship. To me it looked like a bunch of square boxes stacked on top of each other. To get on board we had to walk by crowds of civilians who were family members and friends of departing troops.

Once we boarded the ship, we went down to the troop bay to stow our gear. This ship was a four-stacker; that is to say, the bunks were stacked four high. I had the bottom bunk in my row. It was about a foot from the deck.

After we put our gear away, we all went on deck. The troops who had friends and relatives on the dock crowded the first two decks, all waving and yelling at each other. I had no one to see me off, so I went up to the third deck, which was not crowded, to watch the interaction. Surprisingly, I heard someone call my name several times.

I searched the crowd to see who could be calling my name. I saw a friend of mine who was a schoolmate from Rock Island. His name was John Dingeldein. It was a welcome surprise. He was in California with his sister to visit his brother-in-law, a marine reservist who was activated and stationed at Camp Pendleton, about thirty miles away.

Having John there to see me off is one of my fondest memories. It was the first time I had left home. My friend John has since passed away. I will always remember him.

The E. T. Collins pulled away from the dock after dark, maybe about 10:00 p.m. It was a moonless night, and we could see the harbor lights. The song "Harbor Lights" was popular at that time. Someone had a battery-operated radio. Strangely enough, the song playing was "Harbor Lights." It was an emotional few minutes. I remember the scene vividly—and I still get a bit nostalgic when I hear "Harbor Lights."

It was a fifteen-day voyage across the Pacific. I was sick most of the way. My friend John Fielding, who was in the bunk above me, was well enough to bring me an orange from the mess hall every day. I crossed the Pacific, most of the way, on a dozen oranges.

On Thanksgiving Day I felt better and got in the chow line. When it was my turn to be served, they ran out of turkey, but the mashed potatoes, dressing, and cranberry sauce were great. Turkey or no turkey, it was a better meal than what the troops on the ground in Korea were eating that day.

A couple of days after Thanksgiving, Chinese Communist forces attacked the US Eighth Army and surrounded the First Marine Division, starting the longest military retreat in US history in what was known as the Battle of the Chosin Reservoir, a highlight of Marine Corps history. The marines had to fight their way from the mountains to the sea, destroying a Chinese army in the process. This was one of the greatest achievements in US military history.

The destruction of this Chinese army gave relief to the US Eighth Army in its fight for survival. Of course, we were oblivious to what was happening on the ground in Korea at the time. We had an inkling that we were going to find out, though—and soon.

Those of us on board the E. T. Collins were told that we were going directly to Korea to be replacements for the First Marine Division. The marines practiced aboard ship, firing machine guns, mortars, and rifles off the fantail of the ship. We were told later that we were going to Japan instead of Korea to get cold-weather equipment and clothing.

Stopover in Kobe

We arrived at the seaport of Kobe, Japan, and went to an old World War II Japanese military base, Camp Otsu, thirty miles inland. It had a lot of stucco buildings, in which we lived about ten to a room. But the accommodations were snug and comfortable.

The first day we just got adjusted and familiar with our surroundings. The next day we were given cold-weather clothing, including long underwear, heavy socks, gloves, parkas, fur-like hats, and wool sweaters. We did not receive any military training in Japan, though.

We had one afternoon to see the town but had to be back at midnight. We boarded a train the next day and traveled to a seaport, where we boarded another ship and headed for Pusan, Korea.

When we arrived at Pusan, an Army military band was waiting for us. One of the songs they played was "So Long, It Was Good to Know You." That band knew how to provide a little gallows humor.

Next stop, Korea.

Third Replacement Draft

I arrived in Korea with the third replacement draft the first week of December 1950. Upon arrival we went to the "Bean Patch." This was a very large field that was used for an assembly area for the marine and army divisions near the town of Masan, not far from the port of Pusan. No beans were in this field when we were there, but there might have been at some previous time.

We waited there several days for the First Marine Division to show up. When we arrived, we were lined up and assigned to infantry companies according to the first letter of our last names. If your name started with E, F, or G, you were assigned to Dog Company, Seventh Marines.

Our MOS (military occupation specialty) made no difference in our assignment. Whether someone was formerly an aircraft mechanic, a signalman, a tank driver, an engineer, or an artilleryman didn't matter. Now we were all riflemen.

We were assigned to tents with no cots or stoves. We just lay on the ground with our sleeping bags. Before arriving in Korea I had gone hunting with my .22-caliber rifle. Those little jaunts provided me with as much outdoor training and living as the Marine Corps gave me in its training program.

In one way or another, we were all combat ready when the third replacement draft arrived in Korea. (I modestly admit that the lack of formal training did not hinder us: our combat record proves that we were the best troops in Korea.)

The "Dogs" Arrive

Dog Company survivors of the horrific Chosin Reservoir campaign arrived at the Bean Patch about December 12, 1950, with twelve to fifteen marines and no officers. They looked like men who had been in combat too long—thin, tired, grateful they had survived, and proud of their accomplishments.

I got to be personal friends with some of them as we served together for another six months. Jack Larson, Tom Cassis, Matt Davis, and Larry Hickey became my close friends.

Another of the Chosin Reservoir survivors was a machine gunner whose gun had been overrun by enemy troops. He played dead while a Chinese soldier took his watch and started to take his ring. The Chinese man had trouble getting it off and was about to cut the machine gunner's finger off when a Chinese officer made him stop looting and get moving.

The gunner walked back to marine lines and was among the group of survivors. He told me that he would not go back on the line and said that if he had to, he would shoot himself in the foot—which he did. We helped him to the aid tent. The corpsmen were playing cards and did not even look up. They kept playing cards and said for us to set him in the corner next to another guy who had also shot himself in the foot.

The number of replacements we provided was not enough to fill the ranks, but on the first of January 1951, we got the fourth replacement draft. That gave us about enough to go on line. As I remember, we had a buck sergeant who had been captured on Wake Island during World War II as our company commander (CO). He remained as our CO for the first several weeks, until we received officer replacements.

Of the men in the start-up of the Seventh Marine Regiment, 35 percent were from the Marine Reserve units. Many reservists—including me—had not been to boot camp or had prior military service. Those who were assigned to crew-served weapons held classes and training aboard ship. All in all, the first, second, and third replacement drafts had large groups of men with no prior military training.

Chapter 3
We Meet the Enemy

A Dirty Way to Wage War

In the United Nations drive north from the Pusan Perimeter, troops bypassed the Tenth North Korean Division. The North Koreans (NKs) turned into a guerrilla force that caused havoc among UN forces and the civilian population. They dressed like civilians and blended in with the South Korean refugees to receive cover from them.

We watched the civilians to detect males of military age. We had fairly good luck in finding some of the NKs among the civilians. Some of the NKs were carrying radios they were using to call in mortar fire on us. We sent the captured guerrillas to the rear under escort, where they were placed in a compound for questioning and prisoner of war (POW) camp. Only adult males were captured.

Pohang Guerrilla Hunt—Mid-January to Mid-February 1951

Once the marines integrated the third and fourth replacement drafts, we were up to strength, which allowed us to go on line in an effort to eliminate the hostile enemy troops. This campaign was called the "Pohang Guerrilla Hunt." It should have been named the "freeze and starve hunt." It was a physical nightmare.

Not much combat was involved in the operation. Physically, it was a test of human endurance. The weather was bitterly cold, and the ground was frozen rock solid. We chased NKs from one hilltop to another. We had to dig—or try to dig—into frozen ground, move to the next hilltop, and do it all over again. To make matters worse, we did not eat every day, and supplies did not get to us because we were always on the move.

We were very cold, very tired, and always hungry. Food is fuel, and in the bitter cold we were near freezing. We did not know about wind chill then. The wind was always blowing on the mountaintops, and we soon became aware of what "wind chill" was—even if there was no formal definition for it.

Not Everybody Is Cut Out to Be a Marine

About mid-February 1951 we got a replacement ammo carrier for our machine guns. He wore a camouflage jacket and pants like World War II marines, carried a knife in each boot, and sported a large head that filled his helmet. This man was mean-looking. But it took a lot more than mean looks to be a mean marine.

In addition to looking mean, this replacement had a loud mouth. He claimed that he would not be taking any prisoners once he got into combat. He was going to kill any enemy who surrendered—and no one was going to stop him, he warned us. We laughingly called this somewhat weird newcomer "Marine Mike."

The first firefight in which he was involved began soon after he arrived. Our assignment was to attack an enemy position on a hill that was barren of vegetation. The marines on my left were silhouetted against an overcast sky. Our artillery was giving us supporting fire, which made a swishing noise as it passed overhead. It was just another day at the office for us, and it was a great test for Marine Mike.

I looked over to my left to see how he was doing. He wasn't doing well. Marine Mike was trembling and sobbing. He put his ammo cans down, sat on top of them, and cried like a baby. None of us was especially sympathetic. We relied on one another for support, and he didn't look like he was ready to provide any.

Our platoon leader, a very aggressive individual, shouted to the two marines on either side of Marine Mike. "Grab that man," he ordered. They took Mike's arms. The lieutenant commanded a third marine to fix his bayonet and march Marine Mike up the hill with the ammo. "If he stops, use your bayonet. Do you hear me?" he shouted.

The marine veteran pointed his bayonet and walked up the hill behind Mike. It was strange for the rest of us to see one marine silhouetted against an overcast sky prodding another carrying two cans of ammo as they went into battle. It was like something out of a movie, a la Captain Bligh in *Mutiny on the Bounty* or a French Foreign Legion episode of *Beau Geste.*

We don't know what happened to Marine Mike after that, but we could picture him giving seminars somewhere to a group of admiring listeners as he told them about how he took this hill single-handedly from the Chinese. We knew better.

Let's face it, not everyone is cut out to be a marine—and actions do speak louder than words, especially in combat situations. Most marines who see bayonets in combat see them pointed at them from the front, not the back. Marine Mike was certainly an exception.

February 10, 1951

While on a company combat patrol near Chigadong, Korea, I was in the point-fire team, walking along a narrow path at the base of some very steep rock hills. A frozen creek was about five feet below the path.

While I was walking around a sharp curve, some enemy automatic gunfire hit the marines behind us. The NK troops were disciplined in the fact that they let the point slip by and fired into the center of the column. That was where the forward observers and officers were normally located. Those of us in the point dove into the frozen creek bed. Although we were banged up when we hit the ice, we survived.

One of the marines hit and severely wounded during this action was a forward observer for artillery and a World War II veteran, Lieutenant Charles T. Hinman, a reservist from the Twenty-First Engineer Company, where I got my start. He had been wounded on Okinawa during World War II. Lieutenant Hinman was from my hometown of Rock Island, Illinois. He and the platoon leader were hit at the same time on February 10.

Although Lieutenant Hinman was hit in his thigh and leg, he took over the platoon after the platoon leader was wounded. He directed artillery fire on the enemy position.

He later received a Silver Star for his gallantry in action that day. The citation reads as follows:

> For conspicuous gallantry ... in action against the enemy while serving (as a forward observer) with a Marine infantry company in Korea on February 10, 1951. While proceeding along a narrow uncovered trail on an independent mission near Chigadong, Korea, was taken under fire by deeply entrenched, well camouflaged enemy positions located on the high ground less than 100 yards from the trail. He, with complete disregard for his own personal safety, continually exposed himself to savage enemy automatic weapons fire in order to gain a better position from which to direct artillery fire against the enemy positions. When the platoon leader was seriously wounded, Lieutenant HINMAN took over the platoon and skillfully deployed them and directed their fire against the enemy forces. Though painfully wounded in the thigh and leg, Lieutenant HINMAN refused to be evacuated and continued to direct the platoon and give instructions for the placing of the artillery fire on the enemy positions. His aggressive actions and devotion to duty materially contributed to the success achieved by his company.

February 12, 1951

Night patrols were rare for us. The nighttime belonged to the opposition. Korea had no city lights to bounce off the clouds to give even the faintest illumination. The nighttime in Korea was black or black to blue/black on moonless nights.

We were patrolling one night in a village in pitch-blackness, hoping to find unfriendly troops. We had no luck. Because we had no flashlights, we had to go to the back of the houses, touch the ground-level chimneys, and feel for warmth. If the stack was warm, that meant that the building either was currently occupied or had been recently occupied.

The houses had an ingenious type of radiant heat. A small fire pit was located at one end of the building. The heat and smoke went through the flues under the floor out the back—cooled and then exited through a wooden board chimney at the other end of the house.

As I was walking around to the side of the house, I saw the red glow of a charcoal fire. A human form passed by the red glow toward me. Quickly, I jammed my rifle into the midsection of the form. For some reason, I could not pull the trigger. It was like someone had a hold of my fingers.

The form turned out to be an old man, with an old woman next to him. They did not want to leave their home, so they had stayed behind. It was a miracle that I did not shoot him—or her. But I know this old man had a sore spot in his midsection where I shoved my rifle.

My Life as a Turtle

One night the whole company was moving to a new location under the cover of darkness. We were climbing up a rather steep trail on a moonless night when we stopped to rest. With eighty-plus pounds on our backs, it was difficult getting up if we were sitting on the ground. So we looked for a rock to sit on or something to lean against to make getting up easier.

I saw a blue-black round shape along the side of the trail that looked like a round rock. I sat on this round object and discovered that it was a round bush, which was not built for holding an adult marine carrying a heavy pack. I fell off, tumbled straight down a cliff, and landed on my pack and helmet. If I had not had them on, I may have been killed.

I lay on my back like a turtle with the wind knocked out of me for a while. My buddies did not even realize I had adopted a turtle's life at the bottom of a cliff. They moved on without me.

I knew that I had to catch up with my group, or I would be left behind. I climbed up to the trail with difficulty. My biggest worry was not to startle any of the troops and mistakenly get shot as an enemy combatant. They would shoot me as quickly as they would shoot a turtle. Fortunately, I escaped that fate and rejoined the human world.

Niles Gugliano

Late one afternoon we received word that a large force of NKs was in the next village. We departed hurriedly to intercept them, leaving our parkas and sleeping bags. We wore only our field jackets to lighten our loads and improve our chances in hopes of catching them. As we crossed a mountain stream covered with thin ice, we broke through it into almost waist-deep water.

This stream was at the base of a hill that was about twenty-seven hundred feet high. As we started up the hill, the temperature dropped. The wind started to blow hard, and our clothes began to freeze to us. By the time we got to the top of the hill, dark had set in, and the wind was whipping around at gale force.

The temperature kept dropping, and there was no sign of the enemy. We just sat up on that hilltop and froze. Kids tougher than nails were near tears. We were ruing our decision to leave our parkas and sleeping bags behind.

Several hours later a weapons company showed up with

their parkas and sleeping bags. They did not offer to share their parkas or sleeping bags. They could have shared at least one or the other. Whatever happened to "Semper Fi"? Maybe it applies only in warm weather. ("Semper Fi," a shorter version of the Latin term "Semper Fidelis," is the Marine Corps' motto and is a universal greeting between and among marines. It means, "Always Faithful." Modern marines use a different greeting, "Oorah"—whatever that means. Semper Fi, Oorah ... it makes little difference. Marines are always happy to greet one another with whatever term of respect is in vogue at the time.)

While we were on the hill, I formed a friendship with a marine named Niles Gugliano, who was from St. Louis, Missouri. He had a .38-caliber Colt revolver with a shoulder holster. We were sitting in the cold, freezing together. He told me that he was going over to one of the heavy weapons guys to see if he could trade his Colt for the use of a sleeping bag for the night. He made the trade and came over to me with the sleeping bag. He let me put my feet in it. This sleeping bag was a lifesaver.

Niles paid a heavy price for a rental for about six hours, but it saved our feet. The next morning, when we started to go back down the hill, the other guys could hardly walk. Some could not walk at all. I talked with another marine, Gonzalo Garza, about that night several years after the war and he revealed that he froze his feet and is getting a disability for frozen feet.

Gonzalo was one of many marines with frostbite—which caused more damage to our regiment than the enemy did! We suffered seventeen hundred nonbattle casualties from frostbite, nineteen killed in action (KIA), and fewer than two hundred wounded in action (WIA).

I cannot say enough good things about Niles Gugliano. While we were on this guerrilla hunt, I got the flu or something like it. I could hardly walk, let alone carry my eighty-pound pack. Niles was a horse. He carried me and my pack up those hills and dug our foxhole by himself.

Niles kept me alive. He had a girlfriend named Toni, whom he later married. She was a great Italian girl. She sent him the best food packages, and he shared them with me. Niles has since passed away, but I still stay in touch with Toni. Thanks again, Niles!

Garza, Gugliano, Larson ... Now might be a good time to interject an observation about multiculturalism. In contemporary society it is a hot topic. We did not pay much attention to it as a special thing in Korea. Marines were marines regardless of their ethnic backgrounds. All we cared about was who had our backs. Integration was new then in the US Armed Forces. President Truman had issued an executive order in 1948 ordering all branches of the military to integrate. The marines did not need an executive order to do that—especially when our individual lives depended on men from a variety of ethnic and racial backgrounds.

Fertilizer Business

We were told early in 1951 that we were going to go against Chinese forces at a place near Hoengsong. We heard the US Army's Second Division troops were overrun in this area. About February 15, 1951, the division packed up to leave Masan. This took several days. On the last day we covered up the heads (marine/navy term for outdoor toilets). As we closed the heads, we opened a gold mine for the local farmers, who gathered around to dig this stuff up when we left.

Koreans used human waste to fertilize their crops. We

had to have an armed guard to keep them away until we left the area. I was ordered to be one of the guards to keep the farmers at bay. How embarrassing could it get?

The farmers were sitting on their heels with shovels and buckets. They looked like a bunch of ducks. As the marines passed us to load onto trucks, everyone had some sarcastic and insulting remark to make to me:

"Guard that stuff with your life."

"Shoot to kill."

"You make the marines proud."

"Did you have special training to get that job?"

And on and on.

I said to my marine partner, "I am going over to the farmers to see if I can sell this stuff to the highest bidder."

He said, "Why not? Everything has value."

I went to a farmer, pointed to the stuff, and, in my best Pidgin English, asked, "How muchie won?"

They knew what I meant and broke up into a half-dozen competing groups. A farmer representing one of the groups came over to me holding a wad of won (this is a unit of Korean money) that looked very impressive. So we sold it and guarded it for that group. It was a great feeling as we told the smart-ass, insulting marines all the money we got for the stuff. They were in shock.

The word went up and down the line that we had sold it to the farmers and that they were to stay away, as we were guarding it for the new owners. I wrote home and told my folks that I was in the fertilizer business. They were very proud.

Chapter 4
A Sad Day for the US Army: Operation Killer

Operation Killer

On February 15, 1951, during what was known as Operation Killer, the First Marine Division was on its way to the Chungju/Hoengsong vicinity. The journey was about two hundred miles by rail and truck. We were part of the US Army X Corps, which was placed under the operational control of Major General Bryant E. Moore of the IX Corps.

Unfortunately, General Moore died before Operation Killer ended. He was killed in a helicopter crash on February 24, 1951. Ridgway named Marine General Oliver Prince ("O. P.") Smith as his successor, pending a permanent appointment. Only twice before in Marine Corps history had a marine general commanded significant army units. We were proud of General Smith and felt he was deserving of the command.

General Matthew Ridgway designed Operation Killer to clear the Chinese from the Chip'yong-ni area and the mountains to the southeast, as far as the Som River. He assigned the mission to the IX Corps on February 15.

Chinese forces had taken Hoengsong and had moved into the outskirts of Wonju, a rather large city. At Taegu, we waited for transport to move us to Wonju to be integrated with other units of the IX Corps: the US Army Twenty-Fourth Infantry, the US Army First Cavalry, the Sixth ROK (Republic of Korea) Division, and the Twenty-Seventh British Commonwealth Brigade.

Fighting the French

While we were waiting for our transport, we sat on our packs and watched a French army unit arrive by truck. They stopped and took a break across the road from us. As a small Korean boy walked past them, a French truck driver grabbed off his head a hat the boy was wearing. It had a marine emblem printed on the front.

Marine utility hats with the emblem were in demand by UN troops. The kid tried to get his hat back, but the truck driver kept shoving him to the ground. We watched this happen a few times. Two of us walked over, took the hat from the truck driver, and gave it back to the boy.

The French soldiers started milling round us. Our fellow marines started walking over. The French soldiers got back in their trucks, and the marines went back and sat on their packs. The boy got his hat back and was very happy. We felt good about ourselves, although we would rather have been fighting the Chinese and the North Koreans instead of the French, who were on our side. We would have plenty of time for fighting the real enemy.

The Hills Are Alive—but Not with the Sounds of Music

On March 3, 1951, the Seventh Marines held the high ground south of Hoengsong. We could see our objectives, Hills 536 and 222, in the distance. We took them and started to dig in for the night. Dig in? The ground was frozen solid. Since all we had were light entrenching tools, we knew that we would be lucky to dig a piece of dirt the size of a golf ball.

The First Platoon dug in under some pine trees. The trees looked like evergreen tents with deep pine needles on the ground. We were upset that we were not that lucky. We were on the north slope with no cover; the wind was fierce, and the Chinese were less than welcoming.

Before we could even get a flat spot of ground dug out, Chinese artillery shells started dropping on us. It was heavy stuff, and there was lots of it! We hugged the ground as the shells screamed in and detonated in the frozen earth.

The rock-hard ground released by the shells slammed into our bodies and knocked the wind out of us. We hugged the ground with our elbows and hands between our bodies and the ground to cushion the shock. It was terrifying.

I was told that the artillery barrage lasted about two hours, but to me it seemed like forever. The lush pine-tree cover the First Platoon dug under was reduced to broken and splintered poles stripped of branches. We could see sleeping bags and parkas hanging in the broken trees.

The First Platoon had forty-four men before the artillery fire began. Sadly, when the bombardment ended, the platoon was reduced to fourteen marines. I made a lot of promises to the "Man Upstairs" during the barrage. If I had just kept one of those promises, I would now be living in a monastery.

We learned later that we were shelled by our own guns—at least former guns. The Chinese got the artillery from the army's Fifteenth Field Artillery and the 503rd Artillery Battalion at Hoengsong. This was troubling to us. If the artillery units knew that they were going to be captured, they should have destroyed their weapons before the enemy had the chance to take them. This army artillery was used to kill marines and soldiers a short time later.

The following information is quoted from chapter XIV, "The Battle for Hoengsong," US Army records:

> General Ridgway initially considered these high equipment losses evidence of weak leadership. 10th Corps Commander General Almond was equally disturbed by the heavy loss of equipment, especially the loss of fourteen howitzers by the 15th Field Artillery Battalion and five by the 503rd, and by what he considered excessive personnel casualties among all 2nd Division units. General Ridgway said, "The loss or abandonment to enemy of arms and equipment in usable condition is a grave offense against every member of this command. I shall hereafter deal severely with commanders found responsible and shall expect you to do likewise.

No "Beef" with the Army: We Liberated It!

Dog 7 went into a rest area for a few days to take a well-deserved break and receive replacements from the fifth replacement draft. We dug in next to a food and ammo supply dump that had armed guards patrolling the supplies. When we spotted some boxes of ground beef across the road, two of us got between the guards and "confiscated" a sixty-pound box of frozen ground beef.

There were three twenty-pound packs of ground beef in a box. That would be twenty pounds for each fire team in our squad. Perfect! We started to eat hamburger patties the next day with C ration crackers. It was great! It was the best food we had had in a long time. The sight of hamburger meat would come back to nauseate us.

On March 6, 1951, we went on line and started attacking enemy objectives, which were not even defended. We got a free ride. We were now just a little south and west of Hoengsong, which was our objective the next day. We gathered pinecones to start a small and near-smokeless fire to cook hamburgers. The weather was nice. It was just a few degrees below freezing, and there was no wind.

The next day was a bit tough weather-wise. A light snow that had begun falling during the night continued into early morning. The snow came straight down, and there was no wind. With the pine trees covered with snow, it was very picturesque. We almost forgot we were in a war zone. The feeling did not last long.

Mail Call

We had a sack of mail to drop off to Easy Company as we passed through their positions on our way to Hoengsong, which was in the valley below us. What the hell! We weren't mail-delivery specialists, but we all worked for the government. I'd have been a heck of a lot happier in a post office at the time, though.

When we reached Easy Company, we discovered that they were in a firefight at a heavily defended enemy position on a hill between the two mountain ranges blocking the approach to Hoengsong. As we watched the firefight from a short distance, we could see black figures falling in the snow. Those figures were marines.

Four navy A-1 Skyraiders showed up and "napalmed" the enemy-held hill. The planes took all of five minutes to destroy the enemy positions at a cost of just a few gallons of gasoline. All resistance stopped after the air attack.

We moved out and up the hill, still carrying the mail. Unfortunately, not all the members of Easy Company lived to receive theirs. We walked by some marine casualties covered with ponchos. If I remember correctly, I counted six bodies, who were all victims of chance.

To survive in combat is a matter of luck and timing. For instance, the position that our platoon assaulted the day before was not defended. If the air assault had arrived sooner, there would have been fewer—or no—marine casualties.

As we climbed the hill, we walked through the trenches that the napalm had devastated. It was like a scene out of Dante's *Inferno*. The Chinese defenders were turned into charcoal statues. Luckily for them, they had been killed instantly while aiming rifles toward the attacking marines.

The statues were looking down the barrels of what used to be rifles; the napalm had consumed the wood in the stock. The Chinese in the trenches were also black statues. The Chinese who were away from the trench were burned black and red with their skin rolled up. What a horrible weapon napalm is. An equally horrible scene involving friendly troops awaited us as we moved on.

Massacre at Hoengsong

We dropped off the mail and started down the valley, with my fire team in the point. We walked toward Route 29, an elevated road that went through Hoengsong. In the distance we could see vehicles and artillery lying in different positions along the roadside. As we got closer, we also saw tanks in the ditch.

When we got next to the trucks, we saw bodies—lots of them—stripped to their underwear. Sadly, most of them were American soldiers. We were in shock. We kept asking each other, "How could this happen?"

Tom Cassis, machine-gun section leader in our platoon, said he saw fifty bodies lying in a group in their underwear. The Chinese and North Koreans had stripped the bodies of their cold-weather clothing. The soldiers who surrendered were executed for their cold-weather gear.

The scene was eerie and practically indescribable. In the cold weather, the battlefield had been preserved and frozen in time. We learned that this action had taken place approximately twenty-five days before we arrived—twenty-five days!

The stripped bodies were laid out on the road like railroad ties in near-perfect rows. It looked like a mile of bodies. Most of the dead soldiers may have been killed in combat, but it looked like many were executed. The roadway looked like corduroy with the bodies covered with light snow.

We Lose Our Taste for Hamburger

Some tanks came up the road and stopped where we were standing at the head of the bodies. We milled around in shock at the massacre. Without warning, the lead tank started moving and ran over several bodies before we could stop it. The bright red flesh between the tank treads looked just like the ground beef we stole from the supply dump. We threw the hamburger away. Our appetite for it was gone!

We found out later that the American Support Force 21

(SF 21), which consisted of artillery and infantry with tank support, was attached to the Eighth ROK Division, a command structure that required the total dependence on the ROKs for command and control. The normal command, the Second US Infantry, had no position in the chain of command. SF 21 was comingled, with the ROKs in charge.

This comingling of US and ROK forces was an experiment designed by General Douglas MacArthur's office and enforced by General Almond. This order was suicide for the Americans because the relatively untrained ROKs were completely unreliable. They had a record of bugging out without warning. The US Army had not taken steps to accommodate for that eventuality.

The marines, on the other hand, always had a communication team embedded with the ROKs when they were on our flanks because they were not trustworthy. The ROKs would bug out and not tell anyone on their flanks. Marines always had a radio team in place to check constantly on the ROKs. The Army's Second Infantry Division's Force 21 did not have a team embedded with the ROKs when the ROK's Eighth Division, whose assignment was to protect the Americans, bugged out without telling the Americans.

The US Second Infantry Division was surprised by the collapse of the Eighth South Korean Division and suffered horrible losses on account of the lack of communications with the ROKs, who just ran away and told no one. (*VFW Magazine* published an excellent account of the Hoengsong massacre. The article, "Massacre at Hoengsong," was written by the late Gary Turbak. It is reprinted in this book as Appendix A.)

The Hoengsong Cover-Up

Military authorities later tried to hide the extent of the

casualties in the Hoengsong Massacre, so actual figures are somewhat jumbled. According to US Army records, in chapter XIV, "The Battle of Hoengsong," between midnight on February 11, 1951, and daylight on February 13, 1951, the total of American and Dutch troops killed was 2,018. The Dutch had a one-hundred-man unit as part of Support Force 21. Among them, ninety-nine were killed in action; one was wounded and survived.

In the entire Dutch military history, the action at Hoengsong marked the first time ever that one of its units suffered 100 percent casualties with 99 percent killed. The US Army lost fourteen 105mm howitzers, six 155mm howitzers, 277 crew-served weapons, six tanks, and 280 vehicles.

The ROKs lost six 105mm howitzers and 901 crew-served weapons. ROK casualties amounted to 9,844 killed among the Third, Fifth, and Eighth ROK Divisions. American Army units suffering losses near Hoengsong included the 38th and 17th Infantry; 15th, 503rd, 49th, 96th and 674th Field Artillery Battalions; 82nd Antiaircraft Artillery Automatic Weapons Battalion; and the 187th Airborne Regimental Combat Team (RCT).

Dale Erickson, W/2/7 Remembers

Other marines recall the shock of the Hoengsong discovery. One of them was Dale Erickson, a member of Weapons Company, Second Battalion, Seventh Regiment. (W/2/7). He recalled:

> On March 7, W/2/7 was advancing along with the rest of the Second Battalion of the Seventh Marines to new positions in east-central Korea near the little village of Hoengsong. We had been on the move for two or three hours on foot when we spotted some

American bodies along the road out in a rice paddy. Then we saw another and another, some closer to the road.

As we walked on, more bodies showed up. We had no warning. Then on the road we came upon a military truck with army markings. Checking further, we saw four frozen bodies in the truck—all American soldiers, then more trucks and tanks.

We started seeing bodies all over by the hundreds. Some of them were burned and naked. For every ten American bodies we saw, there was one Chinese body. Government records show that about seven hundred army personnel were killed and maybe executed in this narrow valley. Army records show that 2,018 American and Dutch were killed there February 11–13, 1951. One hundred of the victims were Dutch.

Also lost in this valley were fourteen 105mm howitzers, six 155mm howitzers, six tanks, and 280 vehicles of various types. It is believed that the Chinese forces used some of this captured equipment against us soon thereafter.

I know about this. I was there. We had our own vehicles, trucks, and tanks moving with us on the same road. We came to a place where the road dropped off sharply on one side, and the other side had a rock wall. We saw bodies that were frozen on and beside the road. We had to walk alongside our own trucks and tanks while our vehicles crushed the bodies with wheels and treads, creating a crimson carnage that repulsed the souls of everyone that witnessed it. It was the most horrifying scene that anyone can imagine.

As we walked along, there was not much space between the trucks and tanks and the rock wall. We could not step without stepping on a face or arm or hand. The road was thick with this carnage, and my boots were covered with blood. I could not bear to see this anymore, so I grabbed onto the shoulder of the marine ahead of me, closed my eyes, and stumbled along with him that way for I do not know how long.

I must have blacked out, because I do not remember what happened after that. W/2/7 engaged the enemy two days after we walked through the carnage, and we took some casualties. I did not find this out until later because I had been evacuated to the hospital ship *Repose*.

I woke up on the ship two days later. My body must have reached its limit, and it took me out. It was too much to see. I could not take all the death and dead bodies. I could never get the blood off my boots after that. Part of that experience has stayed with me all of my life.

Investigation of the Massacre

The US Army conducted a postbattle investigation to determine the massacre's cause. (A list of the army casualties in the Hoengsong/Chipyong-ni/Wonju/Chaun-ni area shows the name of every man who was killed there from February 12 through February 14, 1951. It is available at http://www.kwp.org/.) At first, General Almond said that the cause was lack of leadership from the American command. Blame for the fiasco was later placed on the comingling of ROK and US forces, and the finger pointed toward MacArthur and Almond. No doubt the two generals were, at least in part, responsible for us not winning the brutal infantry war in Korea.

The Korean massacre at Hoengsong was inflicted as the result of enemy action, but the massacre was set up by a military failure from the American high command: General

MacArthur and General Almond. Putting American forces under the command of incompetent and unreliable South Korean army leadership was an untried experiment doomed to failure, thereby sacrificing the lives of thousands of American troops on the altar of stupidity.

MacArthur and Almond would not admit that they were responsible in any measure for the massacre. They reversed the results of the investigation, putting the blame instead on General Choi Yong Hee, commander of the Eighth ROK Division. The Chinese forces crushed the Eighth ROK Division and then ran along both sides of elevated Route 29 to set up roadblocks and trap UN forces.

When the blame for the Hoengsong Massacre pointed back to MacArthur and Almond, they hid this atrocity from the public. Certainly, it wasn't the first time in history American soldiers had been massacred. Only a few years earlier, during World War II on December 16, 1944, near Malmedy, a Belgian town in the Ardennes, German SS troops murdered eighty-one American soldiers during the Battle of the Bulge. But that atrocity was in every newspaper and on every radio station in the country.

The killings at Malmedy were the worst single atrocity committed against American troops in Europe during World War II, and the world knew about it. Six years and two months later in Korea, on February 12 and 13, 1951, about twelve thousand American, South Korean, and Dutch soldiers were killed in combat or executed in a single battle, yet this massacre has been kept a secret all these years.

Payback

During the offensive in the spring and early summer of 1951, we fought Chinese soldiers wearing US Army jackets with the Second Division patch. We reached into the pockets of the dead Chinese soldiers wearing those jackets and took out letters and pictures from the folks at home in which they discussed the plans that were in store when the soldiers returned home. Those letters brought tears to our eyes as we read them and looked at the pictures. It was flat-out heart-wrenching.

We wanted so much to write to the friends and families of these US soldiers and say, "We killed the SOBs who executed your dad, son, husband, brother, or friend." We were told not to write to the folks at home because it would just create problems. Rather, we were instructed to turn the letters in to company officers. They, in turn, would forward them to Graves Registration. To my knowledge, all of us did as we were told.

That did not compensate for the loss of over 2,040 American soldiers, however—and my heart breaks for them and their family members to this day.

Chapter 5
The March Continues

I Wouldn't Want to Be a Grenadier

Dog 7 had three rifle platoons we used as individual combat units. Each platoon was looking for unfriendly forces wherever they might be found. About midnight on March 10, 1951, First Platoon radioed Third Platoon for assistance because they were being attacked by enemy forces. While going to help the First Platoon, the Third Platoon was attacked by Chinese grenadiers.

These grenadiers had a distasteful job—at least for them. They belonged to a unit of the Chinese army whose sole purpose was to throw grenades. They were followed by infantry soldiers with automatic weapons trying to punch holes in the opposing forces to get behind them and destroy them.

Sergeant Jack Larson was the squad leader of the squad the grenadiers hit. The Chinese could not have picked a worse adversary. Sergeant Larson was calm, cool, and effective. He was seriously wounded by grenades. In spite of his wounds,

Larson kept arranging his squad in various defensive positions that stopped the superior enemy forces. For saving his platoon, Sergeant Larson was awarded the Navy Cross.

Sergeant Larson's Navy Cross Citation

The President of the United States takes pleasure in presenting the Navy Cross to Sergeant Jack F. Larson, United States Marine Corps Reserve, for service as set forth in the following citation:

> For extraordinary heroism while serving as a Squad Leader of Company D, Second Battalion, Seventh Marines, First Marine Division (Reinforced), in action against enemy aggressor forces south of Hongch'on, Korea, on 11 March 1951. Observing an excellent avenue of approach leading directly into the forward portion of his position while arranging the defense of newly won high ground following a bitter fight, Sergeant Larson conducted one fire team to an area covering the lane of access and, while digging in, was forced to withdraw when a hail of hostile automatic-weapons and small-arms fire rendered the site temporarily untenable. Occupying an alternate position until darkness, he returned to complete his defensive preparations despite continued enemy fire. When a large hostile force subsequently launched a vigorous assault, inflicting serious wounds on his comrades and himself, he braved intense enemy fire to remain at his post and, by skillfully manning his weapon, prevented the hostile troops from penetrating the sector and jeopardizing the entire company position. Despite severe pain from his wounds, he single-handedly withstood all enemy assaults for approximately two hours and, after the

hostile assailants had been repulsed and his wounded comrades had received aid, consented to submit to treatment for his own wounds. By his inspiring leadership, indomitable fighting spirit and steadfast devotion to duty, Sergeant Larson contributed materially to the security of the company position, thereby upholding the highest traditions of the United States Naval Service.

The Chinese Win the Race; We Win the Place

As March 11, 1951 arrived, we were north of Hoengsong on a platoon combat patrol, once again looking for unfriendly forces. As darkness approached, we thought about digging into a defensive position for the night.

We approached the top of a mountain where all the ridges ran together into a large flat area. Up from this flat area was a long trench line that covered all the ridges. As we stared at the trenches for a bit, we saw a brown wave of Chinese troops running down the hill toward the trenches. We dropped our packs and started running toward the same trench.

It was a race for survival. We did not want to be caught in the open with the Chinese in the trenches shooting at us. The Chinese were lying back, expecting artillery fire and air attacks, followed by an infantry assault. They didn't have to worry about any of them coming from us. We did not have any artillery or air support.

When the Chinese figured this out, they came out of hiding to get to the trench. They beat us to the elevated trench line but not by much. They had a problem deflecting their rifles down on us, as we were too close to them.

We talked about this event among ourselves later. Some marines said they pulled rifles out of Chinese hands. Several of us got to the end of the trench line, jumped in undetected, and shot into the Chinese. They started to fall over like dominoes. The Chinese soldiers were trapped and could only run back from us, but the high and wide trench held them captive.

It was such an adrenaline rush for us that it is hard to remember all that took place in those few minutes. Things were a blur. It was fortunate that we did not shoot one another.

I remember cutouts in the trench line where troops could seek shelter from air attacks. The Chinese started diving into the cutouts as if they were diving into a pool. I remember saying to myself, "I wonder where they think they are going?" It was kind of funny.

The Chinese soldiers kept falling over in front of us, and we kept running over them like sacks of potatoes. It seemed as if when we shot into them, two or more fell over. We got to the end of the trench very quickly.

Looking down the trench, we could see Chinese soldiers in their brown quilted cold-weather uniforms covering the bottom of the trench. It was getting dark, so we started to dig in for the night. This run through the trench line was such an adrenaline rush I could not sleep when it was my turn to do so. We could not wait for daylight to check our work.

Chinese Possums

At daybreak we walked over to the trench. To our great surprise, we could see the bottom of the trench! There were bodies, but not as many as we thought. Our platoon leader, an efficient and gung ho officer, walked by us. He was visibly upset and highly agitated.

He asked, "Do you want to know where they are? I will

tell you. At daybreak, they were at the bottom of the hill walking around the colonel's tent with their hands up trying to surrender."

We could visualize this. It was hilarious, and we started to laugh. He said that it was not funny. He could get court-martialed for this because the Chinese could have wiped out our command post.

We did our best to stop laughing, but he just got more upset and said to us, "You have bayonets. Start using them. I want all bodies stuck with bayonets! Do you hear me?"

When he left, the marine I was with said, "He must be kidding." He was not going to stick any Chinese with his bayonet because he used it to open his jelly can.

I agreed. We believed our platoon leader had been watching too many John Wayne movies.

In taking this trench line, two marines were killed and six were wounded. That was not many; however, any loss of life was tragic. Considering the many Chinese troops that we engaged, this was not considered excessive.

We did good work that day, but we did not get any "atta boys." Instead, we got chastised because many of the Chinese who we thought were dead had played possum and went down the hill during the night and tried to surrender. The colonel was not happy, and he did some butt-chewing. This was passed on to us.

MacArthur Could Have Been a Five-Star Vaudeville Headliner

On March 17, 1951, we went into division reserve. This was good because we got to be in camp with the general. We had not been in division reserve before. Mostly, we had been in battalion reserve, which had few creature comforts.

Sometimes we just went back to where the artillery was. We listened to outgoing artillery all night long, but at least it was going in the right direction.

We were in the rest area and dug in next to the army's Ninety-Second Armored Artillery Battalion, whose members called themselves "the Red Devils." They were giving us artillery support. We were next to a creek when several army flatbed trucks pulled up.

Soldiers got out and started setting up cameras on the flatbed trucks and the creek banks, with one in the water. Then a cavalcade of jeeps showed up. There, in the lead jeep, wearing dark glasses, a crushed-down hat, and a trench coat, was General MacArthur, who was known to us as "Back Track Mac."

The general's jeep entered the shallow creek and stopped for several minutes. The cameras started rolling, and flashbulbs flashed. Then his jeep turned around and left with the trucks following him. A week later his picture was on the front page of the military newspaper *Stars and Stripes.* The headline read, "General MacArthur visits the front." The general should have been in vaudeville.

When we got to the reserve area, we were told we were going to be guarding the general's compound. This compound consisted of four or five tents, most with heating stovepipes out the tops. It looked nice and homey.

We slept under the stars in rain or snow with nothing but ponchos for a roof. The compound had a snow-like fence around it made of strips of wood held together with wire. It was very easy to roll up and move. We soon found that one of the tents we were guarding was a food supply tent. This was like making Jesse James night watchman at the train depot. We made plans ...

Our New Diet Plan

Our plan was simple: the squad on duty would direct the requisition group to the food tent and point out the specials. The first night we requisitioned canned ham, bacon, butter, red-raspberry jam, fresh bread, milk, apples, oranges, and fresh eggs. This was the food of dreams for a marine infantryman, especially apples and oranges. This food was the best I had had since I arrived in Korea.

We did not have field kitchens like the army had—at least not for the marine infantry. We had a very primitive lifestyle. In our chow line they served us warmed-up beans, corned beef hash, beef stew, and canned peaches or fruit cocktail. The food was just like our C rations, only from larger cans.

The C rations were left over from World War II. They had been frozen during winter and heated in the summer for seven or eight years. It turned this food into garbage. The chocolate bar was turned into a white powder. C rations were our staple, and we felt lucky if we had enough of them.

About mid-1951, C rations were changed from World War II silver cans to new C rations in olive-drab-colored cans with some good stuff, such as chicken and rice, hamburger and potatoes with gravy, sausage patties, spaghetti with meatballs, ham and beans, and ham with lima beans. It was new, and it was pretty good.

Later, we got field kitchens when we went into reserve, and we got fresh milk, fresh fruit, and bread and butter. It was a long time coming. We all sat around a small fire eating the general's food and agreed that he had a great pantry. I must have eaten five or more ham and egg sandwiches on fresh bread, washing them down with milk and orange juice. This was without exception my fondest memory of my stay in Korea.

Consideration for the Cook

That night was my turn to be part of the "requisition team." I received orders for pancake mix and maple syrup. After dark we went up to the guard in front of the compound and gave him a password, such as "Jesse James" or "Cole Younger." We got a countersign and learned that the general's cook was in the tent sleeping on a cot next to the stove. We carefully filled our orders and quietly left so as not to wake the cook.

The next morning, we were gathered around our cooking fire enjoying pancakes with real butter and maple syrup with bacon on the side, washing it down with milk, when a tall, stern-looking first lieutenant and two marines showed up. They had like-new utilities on, and we looked like mutts next to them.

The lieutenant said in a commanding voice, "I am not going to ask where or how you got all this food. I am ordering you to take it back. *Now!* You people could be in a lot of trouble."

Someone asked, "Do we have to take all the food back?"

The lieutenant said, "I want everything that has not been opened returned," which for us was a great deal, because we got to keep the leftovers. We returned the food while getting dirty looks from the two cooks. Needless to say, we lost our positions as perimeter guards for the general's compound.

Chapter 6
Back to the War

No Rest for the Weary—or the Fresh

We "rested" for less than a week. On March 24, 1951, Dog 7 went back on line, once again attacking and pushing the commies back. We dug in for the night in two-man foxholes with 50 percent watch, setting out bobby traps with two-man outposts in front of each platoon to prevent enemy infiltration. The next day we did it all over again.

Everyone Has a Warped Sense of Humor

Early spring was upon us. The weather was getting warmer, and digging foxholes was getting easier as the frost left the ground. We were occupying ground that American troops had occupied in the past. Consequently, we had predug foxholes on the north slope, which saved us lots of digging.

We found the perfect predug foxhole; it was wide, long, and deep. We put our sleeping bags in place and started to get comfortable. The weather was getting warmer, and there was a terrible stench about the place.

The Chinese and North Koreans buried their dead on the ground where they fell, covering them with branches, leaves, and sometimes a little dirt. That way, we could not count their casualties.

We started to police the area and found a dead Chinese soldier under some branches not far from us. We moved him downwind and went back to our dugout, but the smell got worse.

My foxhole buddy was Matt Davis, from south-central Texas. He was an interesting person. Matt's family was formerly from Missouri. After the Civil War his family was on the wrong side of history, so they moved to Texas.

Matt was a historian as well as a philosopher. No matter how cold, hungry, and tired we were, Matt could reach back in history and compare us and our hardships with another group of soldiers long past who had had it much worse than we did. He made us feel that we were part of a military tradition steeped in a thousand years of history.

I said, "Someday they will be talking about us." That was a scary thought.

Matt the Magnet

Matt's philosophy and uncomplaining attitude lifted our spirits and helped create the bonding that combat soldiers can relate to. And, if anyone had a lot to complain about, it was Matt. He was a magnet for enemy bullets.

Matt was wounded at the Chosin Reservoir in November 1950. I met Matt when he was released from the hospital in February 1951.

Matt was wounded for a second time on June 10, 1951.

When he was released from the hospital, he was assigned to a rear-echelon unit with all the comforts of home. Matt demanded that he be returned to Dog/7 to live in the dirt with all the dangers of combat infantry. Matt was a true warrior.

About September 1951, Matt was wounded for the third time. He was hit by machine-gun fire and gravely wounded. I helped put him on a helicopter that was taking the wounded to the rear for medical treatment.

The medical corpsman who was there at the time said that Matt would be dead before he could get to the aid station. By some miracle, Matt lived—for another forty-seven years, in fact. But while he was with us, he was a steadying influence on our morale, which we greatly appreciated and badly needed.

Telltale Toilet Paper

We were told we would be staying in the place we currently held for several more days as we waited for our flanks to catch up. We started recon patrolling in front of our positions up to the start of the next mountain range. Identifying the enemy was easy: we could tell if it was the Chinese or North Koreans who had been there because when they relieved themselves they did not bury their business. Instead, it was a gift to the local farmers to put on their fields. The Chinese used toilet paper, and the North Koreans did not.

Of course, we did not want to seem unappreciative for the enemy's kindness. We left them little "gifts" in return, such as our worst-tasting cans of C rations. For me, it was the beef stew. This World War II ration was so old it tasted like candle wax.

We left a few cans of C rations lying about but took one empty can, slipped a grenade in the can (which was a tight fit), and pulled the pin. The tight fit kept the spoon from flying off and arming the grenade. We then set the can straight up, bottom open.

When someone picked up the can, the grenade fell out, and the spoon fell off, activating the grenade. The commies had about four seconds for small talk—and they never got to taste the C rations, which were almost as lethal as the grenades.

Three-Man Foxhole

Back in our foxhole, the stench was getting unbearable. We got out of our dugout, started moving leaves around, and saw a small rubber tip sticking out of the floor of our foxhole. We dug around the object with our shovel and dug up a foot—then a leg with a Chinese quilted uniform on it. We had been sleeping on top of a dead Chinese soldier.

I said, "Matt, we have a three-man foxhole but only two of us are keeping watch." We moved next door with a freshly dug foxhole, and we threw the dirt on top of the Chinese soldier. We were victims of a stinking Chinese dirty trick.

Winning the Hearts and Minds of the People

There were other patrols of interest that run together in my mind as to their timing. I know that after we took an objective, we started to patrol the villages and the territory around our recently acquired property. The marines had a fetish for patrols. We wanted to know what was out there in our front yard.

One cloudy and cold day on patrol we came upon a village. The people were in a long row in front of their huts. Some of the women and children were crying uncontrollably. The entire group of village people was kneeling on the bare ground. We had no idea why they were behaving so strangely.

I went up to a young boy and handed him a stick of gum. The boy had never seen or chewed gum before. He stared at it for a second or so, not knowing what it was. His mother, kneeling next to him, hit him for his hesitation. The boy got the hint. He put the gum in his mouth, wrapper and all, and started chewing.

No doubt he figured he might as well die chewing some strange substance, wrapper and all. We learned quickly that the Chinese had told the villagers the Americans would kill them if they came to their village. We put that idea to rest quickly. We gave them some of our meager rations and left as friends.

We patrolled the next village a few miles away, and the people came out to meet us timidly. They were very nervous and scared. The commies had told them the same thing about Americans.

We calmed them down and asked them about several males of military age whose legs were amputated below the knees. They were sitting on some straw. They said they were Chinese soldiers that had had frozen limbs. The villagers took them in and amputated their feet and legs without anesthesia.

The sight of these young men was disturbing, even to us battle-hardened marines. We walked over to them and gave them our C ration cigarettes. The Chinese soldiers knew the meaning of tough times. We left this village as friends.

The Casualties of War Extend beyond the War Fighters

On another patrol in late spring or early summer 1951, we went into a farmhouse to check it over. Inside we saw a deceased woman and her two children, each of whom appeared to be about three years old. They looked like twins dressed in their finest clothing.

The mother was also dressed in her finest clothing. They were lying in a bed under a fancy quilt with the mother in the center. It looked to us as if they had died from cholera.

In the next room was a man hanging by his neck, an apparent suicide. We guessed he did not want to live without his family. This, to all of us, was very sad.

War does not discriminate when it comes to victims or the manners in which they die.

Chapter 7
A Hero on Hill 430: Richard DeWert Earns the MOH

Run, Fred, Run

Around the last week of March 1951, our platoon leader asked me to be his runner, the sometimes-unlucky person who carried dispatches from one unit to another under combat conditions. It was a necessary—but extremely dangerous—job. I did not want this job because I had bonded with my buddies in my four-man fire team. (Runners are a thing of the past nowadays. Soldiers have other highly technological means of communication—and they don't even use foxholes much anymore.)

There were three of these units per squad—if it was up to full strength, which we generally were not. We bonded with our buddies in the fire team. They were our family, and for me accepting the job of runner would be like leaving home.

In my heart, I knew had to take the job of runner. Some other marine took my place in my fire team. I was not happy.

On April 1 we were told that our Seventh Marine Regiment was to be placed under the operational control of the commanding general of the US Army's First Cavalry Division. We were now in the army! If I had wanted to be in the army, I would have joined it.

We told Richard DeWert that from now one we would have to call him "the medic," like in the army and not "the corpsman," like in the marines. He said that would be okay and wanted to know if we would now get cherry pie with our C rations! This was a standing joke. (While the army has its own medics, the Marine Corps relies on US Navy medical personnel called corpsmen for battlefield support. Inevitably, they are all called "Doc" by their marine buddies, who would not think of going into combat without them.)

Marine Corps or Army—Nothing's Changed

On April 5 we crossed the 38th parallel, which was the dividing line between North and South Korea. It was a joint operation between Easy and Dog Companies. We took the ridge toward the south; Easy Company took the ridge toward the west. We were both going up to the same objective, Hill 430.

This hill was a piece of ground about thirteen hundred to fourteen hundred feet high—an easy climb. The day was bright to partly cloudy. As we climbed the hill, the cloud formation turned into fog, which at times made visibility very limited. Then the fog would clear, and the hill would be very bright.

The enemy usually defended a hill by placing forces where the ridges met at its top. That way all approaches could be covered by their gunners. My old fire team was in the point.

We could hear heavy machine-gun fire and grenade explosions near the top when the fire team neared it.

I was about forty yards from the point with our platoon leader, as I was his runner. In most cases we went up the ridges almost single file because of the narrow paths along them. The fog had moved in again, and visibility was very limited. Bullets from the almost invisible enemy were clipping tree branches. The fog worked both ways; we could not see one another, so we got very close to each other. I had moved next to the marines who were being sheltered by a small ridge not more than two feet high.

The machine-gun fire was heavy and continuous. Along with the noise of battle, we could hear someone screaming obscenities such as, "You dirty sons of bitches," over and over. Suddenly, the fog shifted, and it was very bright. It was like a movie—but one that would have a bad ending.

I could see DeWert almost falling on top of the marine doing the cussing. The corpsman had gone to the aid of the cussing marine, who was shot in the knees and was in great pain and shock. A short way from the fallen DeWert was a bunker with the enemy machine gunners. It had a large aperture from which the gunners were covering all approaches. Corpsman DeWert had gone under enemy fire four times to aid wounded marines during the firefight, and he had been shot multiple times.

Without thinking, I ran up to the bunker, slid on my knees, and shot into the faces that I could plainly see. Then I checked on DeWert, who was dead. I went to the still-cussing wounded marine. I dragged him behind a rock formation and out of harm's way—but not out of earshot.

He called me every cussword he could think of. A tough, no-nonsense corpsman by the name of Fred Hardy told this wounded marine that if he didn't shut his mouth, he was going to drag his ass back up the hill and leave him there.

We charged up the hill as a group, past the now-silent bunkers, and up the trail that led to a group of Chinese riflemen. These Chinese, who were protecting the bunker and shooting at us, had to be the world's worst marksmen. They bugged out before we could get to them.

When we gathered up our dead and wounded, I saw Chuck Curley, one of our machine gunners, now a stretcher bearer, lift DeWert's body onto a stretcher. Water was running out of DeWert's canteen from the bullet holes in it.

It was a sad day. I also remember the dead from my old fire team being placed on stretchers. I looked at the marine who took my place; he was dead. Fate had traded his life for mine.

I have mixed emotions about the trade to this day. I feel some consolation in the fact that if I had been killed, the possibility was not remote that the Chinese would have killed more marines that day.

Corpsman Courageous

Hospitalman Third Class Richard DeWert, US Navy, joined Dog/7 the first week in March 1951. Richard had a combat history prior to joining Dog/7. I will write about him as I knew him when he served in Dog 7, until he was killed on April 5, 1951. DeWert was a nineteen-year-old sailor, good-looking and well built. He was serious by nature and did not go for all the marine/navy horseplay that was prevalent at this time. On March 10, 1951, Sergeant Jack Larson's patrol was ambushed by Chinese grenadiers, whose sole purpose was to throw grenades, followed by the Chinese infantry. Sergeant Larson and his squad beat back the ambush after suffering almost 100 percent casualties; among the wounded was Hans Schultz, a World War II combat vet who lost an eye. HM3 Richard DeWert had a busy night on March 11, 1951.

Just before dark that night, Dog/7's Third Platoon, while on combat patrol north and west of Hoengsong, on a mountaintop, ran into a large group of Chinese soldiers who were about to ambush our patrol. We beat back the ambush against unbelievable odds. That was a precursor to two busy nights for HM3 Richard DeWert.

March 12–13, 1951

"Doc" DeWert set up office to care for the sick and bruised after two days of combat. Doc was busy. When I got to see him, I told him I had dirt in my eye. He opened his medical kit, which was organized according to the colors of the rainbow: Yellow Bayer aspirin tablets, white cans of Johnson & Johnson Band-Aids, red bottles of cough syrup. I said, "Hey, Doc, your kit looks like a drugstore back home. Do you have any candy bars?" He said he had them on order. I said, "Put me down for a case." All the other corpsmen I had gotten to know had all their medication wrapped up in olive-drab wrappers. Richard DeWert's kit was a taste of home.

On our left flank, a US Army outfit moved in during the early morning hours. It always fascinated the marines by how much stuff they had and how they got resupplied. For food they had civilians in blue uniforms carrying large containers of food. I was next to Richard during one of the army's food resupply missions. We talked about what was in the large canisters. We named all kinds of food, and someone mentioned cherry pie. This is when the conversation got misty-eyed. Richard said, "Cherry pie is to die for."

An Unexpected Reminder of Home

While I was checking the guns in the bunker after the battle, I found out that they were two water-cooled .30-caliber Brownings made at the Rock Island Arsenal in Illinois. The guns had brass tags affixed that read, "US ARMY." Ironically, Rock Island was my hometown. The Chinese were shooting at us with weapons my friends and neighbors had made.

Possibly, the guns had been taken near Hoengsong about a month earlier when the Army's Second Division and supporting troops were sent to support the ROK troops, who had left and told no one. The troops had been overrun and massacred by divisions of Chinese Communists. The Easy Company commander, who was on the west ridge, radioed our platoon leader and thanked him for taking out the machine guns that had pinned down his company.

Welcome praise? Yes. Was it consolation for the sacrifices of men like Richard DeWert, my fire-team buddies, the man who took my place, and others whose remains we put in body bags that day? Not at all.

Men who fight, bleed, and suffer the agonies of battle find no comfort in such detached deliberation. They are too involved with their vivid and tragic memories.

The Fight to Get DeWert a Medal of Honor Begins

For some unexplained reason, HM3 DeWert did not immediately receive recognition for his heroic sacrifices. To me and others this was troubling. About mid-April 1951, Dog 7 got two new replacement officers, both World War II veterans: Captain Alvin Mackin and Second Lieutenant Lealon Wimpee.

Mackin, our new company commander, had served in the

Marine Air Corps. Lieutenant Wimpee, an infantry enlisted man who had been wounded on Okinawa, was our new platoon leader. Eventually, they initiated the process to rectify that oversight. They were like breaths of fresh air, especially after Captain Mackin introduced himself personally to each member of the company. This was unheard of in our experience. Captain Mackin was like a big brother to us, and we bonded instantly with him.

A day or so after Lieutenant Wimpee took charge of the platoon, he asked ten of us to go with him to act as an honor guard for a ceremony honoring a forward observer who was getting a citation for valor. The lieutenant wanted us to all be wearing utilities that matched. This was difficult, since we got our clothing from a pile of laundered clothing from all branches of service, and there were no men's clothing stores nearby.

When we took showers, which was not all that often, we just took off our dirty clothes and put them in the pile with other soiled clothes. Then we went to a clean pile of clothes and put on anything that fit, stripes and all. One marine private got to be an army first sergeant by just taking a shower!

Changing clothes was essential for us. Without access to new clothes we would be fighting naked, which would have scared the Chinese almost as much as our weapons did—maybe more.

Mountain warfare was hard on the knees and seats of pants. The Marine Corps fought its wars on a budget. We were like Coxey's (or Cox's) Army. Our preferred article of clothing was an Australian wool sweater, but that day we swapped clothing so ten of us had matching utilities.

(In 1894, when poor people walked everywhere, one Jacob

Sechler Coxey—then the respectable Republican mayor of Massillon, Ohio—marched a ragged army of one hundred men from his hometown to Washington to get the government to do something about hard times (*Time*, Monday, January 18, 1932). A similar group, led by Father James Renshaw Cox, a Roman Catholic priest, marched on Washington for the same purpose.)

At the ceremony, the forward observer received a citation for valor by putting himself in harm's way after being assigned to Dog Company and calling devastating mortar fire on enemy positions.

While we were walking back to our unit after the ceremony, I did a slow burn. I thought about Richard DeWert, who had died a real hero but received no recognition for his sacrifice. This living forward observer received a citation for putting himself in harm's way by being assigned to Dog 7. It seemed to me that, if being assigned to Dog 7 put him in enough danger to deserve a citation, all Dog Company marines should get citations for valor for being assigned with each other. We were all in harm's way.

After I got to know Lieutenant Wimpee, I asked him if it was possible for him to recommend someone for a citation who was killed before he arrived. He replied in the affirmative, but he had a few questions. I told him about Richard DeWert, who we all felt died a real hero but, for some reason, had received no recognition.

First, Lieutenant Wimpee wanted to know who the platoon leader was when DeWert was killed, why he had not written up the citation, and whether there were any witnesses. I said that I could answer all but the second question.

I told him the story of DeWert. Most importantly, I said,

I had witnesses to DeWert's action. The lieutenant told me to get them, and he would write a citation for DeWert.

My two other witnesses were Private First Class John Alseth and Private First Class Robert Gentry. Both had seen DeWert when he was wounded and still trying to save marines.

The four of us sat in the dirt and wrote an account of Richard's heroic actions. Lieutenant Wimpee gave the report to Captain Mackin, who signed it and sent it up the line. Ultimately, DeWert received the Medal of Honor, posthumously. These two men of action, Captain Mackin and Lieutenant Wimpee, had come along at just the right time as far as we were concerned. As a result of their efforts, Richard B. DeWert received the Medal of Honor he had so justly deserved.

Medal of Honor Citation—Richard David DeWert:

> For conspicuous gallantry and intrepidity at the risk of his life above and beyond the call of duty while serving as a HM3, in action against enemy aggressor forces. When a fire team from the point platoon of his company was pinned down by a deadly barrage of hostile automatic weapons fired and suffered many casualties, HM3 DeWert rushed to the assistance of one of the more seriously wounded and, despite a painful leg wound sustained while dragging the stricken marine to safety, steadfastly refused medical treatment for himself and immediately dashed back through the fire swept area to carry a second wounded man out of the line of fire. Undaunted by the mounting hail of devastating enemy fire, he bravely moved forward a third time and received another serious wound in the shoulder after discovering that a wounded marine had already died. Still persistent

> in his refusal to submit to first aid, he resolutely answered the call of a fourth stricken comrade and, while rendering medical assistance, was himself mortally wounded by a burst of enemy fire. His courageous initiative, great personal valor, and heroic spirit of self-sacrifice in the face of overwhelming odds reflect the highest credit upon HM3 DeWert and enhance the finest traditions of the U.S. Naval Service. He gallantly gave his life for his country.

Sergeant Gonzalo Garza, a member of D/7, wrote to me that if Richard DeWert had not received the Medal of Honor for his actions on April 5, 1951, the sacrifices that Dog Company made that day would be just "dust in the wind." This is so very true.

Hundreds of firefights, patrols, and battles take place in a war. Most just become fading memories in the minds of the survivors. Those participants killed are registered in the casualty reports. Their names also will fade to the backwaters of history. Over time they will be remembered collectively on Memorial Day as the "war dead."

Their personal sacrifices and pain will be, just as Garza suggested, dust in the wind.

Other Tributes to DeWert

Special thanks are due to Charles Curley for his efforts in raising a million-dollar scholarship fund at Pepperdine University in Richard DeWert's honor. Curley did this unilaterally and out of his own pocket. This gave the DeWert legacy legs. Curley also started an endowment fund at Pepperdine University in Colonel Alvin Mackin's honor, again out of his own pocket.

Master Chief Fred Kasper, US Navy, pulled strings and got the navy/marines to name the clinic at Bridgeport, California, the Richard DeWert Clinic. The navy hospital at Newport, Rhode Island, was also named the Richard DeWert Medical Clinic. (See Appendix B for Kasper's story about Richard DeWert.)

Also, a ship, USS *DeWert* (FFG 45), is named in his honor. A school, a highway, and more are named after him. My own "claim to fame" is being the catalyst to get Richard DeWert the Medal of Honor. I am happy to know that Richard DeWert will receive recognition for generations to come.

Those of us who served in Dog Company, Seventh Marines will also share in this recognition with pride. Without all concerned acting in unison to get Richard the recognition he deserved, he would have been just another dead sailor in a box. Dog Company, Seventh Marines received one Medal of Honor during the Korean War, and it was not for a marine. It was for a sailor. They are one and the same when it comes to corpsmen.

My Silver Star

Just for the record, I earned a Silver Star, the nation's third-highest combat military decoration, for my actions that day, April 5, 1951. I am proud of that—but not nearly as proud as I am that I got the proverbial ball rolling to get Richard B. DeWert the medal he so richly deserved and earned.

Silver Star Citation—Fred Frankville

SILVER STAR

SECRETARY OF THE NAVY

The President of the United States takes pleasure in presenting the Silver Star Medal to Private First Class

> FREDRICK P. FRANKVILLE, United States Marine Corps Reserve, for service as set forth in the following citation:
>
> For conspicuous gallantry and intrepidity while serving as a Rifleman of Company D, Second Battalion, Seventh Marines, First Marine Division (Reinforced), in action against enemy aggressor forces in Korea on 5 April 1951. When his unit was subjected to intense and accurate hostile automatic-weapons and small-arms fire from cleverly concealed bunkers, during an attack against a strongly defended enemy hill position, Private First Class FRANKVILLE fearlessly charged forward through the heavy fire to aid a wounded comrade lying in an exposed position within a few feet of the enemy and boldly delivered point-blank fire into the aperture of a hostile bunker. Despite hand grenades bursting around him, he succeeded in carrying his wounded companion to a safe position and quickly rejoined his platoon in the final assault to overrun the enemy emplacements. By his outstanding bravery, inspiring initiative and courageous devotion to duty, Private First Class FRANKVILLE contributed materially to the success of his company and upheld the highest traditions of the United States Naval Service.

Hearts Filled with Pain

In August 1951, long after the April battle in which Richard DeWert was killed, our new company commander, Captain Alvin Mackin, wrote to the corpsman's mother to express his condolence. DeWert's foster mother wrote in her response:

Dear Captain Mackin,

Receiving your letter was most comforting. Knowing that Richard died so honorably eases, somewhat, the pain that will always remain in our hearts. Although we are not his natural parents, being childless, we loved him more than words can describe.

He was brought up under atrocious conditions by a mother who was only concerned about herself. Richard had to fend for himself from earliest childhood. He could have gone just as bad as he was good, but God in His infinite wisdom gave him a pure heart. He came to us, we thought at the time quite by accident; but now we know different. God sent him to us so that we could shower him with the love and affection that he never had received in early childhood. He, in turn, returned that love and affection on us that we also never received from a child of our own.

We were never able to adopt him legally as his mother would never relinquish him. His and our big aim in life was for him to become twenty-one so that we could adopt him legally. It was not His will that it be so; however we will never forget Richard's memory and will always carry it in our hearts.

Knowing that you are burdened with many and tedious duties, we thank you from the bottoms of our hearts for taking the time to write us such a comforting letter.

Respectfully yours,

Mrs. Albertina Roy

Corpsman Honoring Corpsman

Fred Kasper, a senior chief corpsman in the United States Navy, learned of the heroic efforts of fellow corpsman Richard David DeWert many years after DeWert died on the battlefield. Kasper wrote the following tribute in honor of fellow corpsman Richard David DeWert:

A Corpsman's Reflection

I woke up yesterday morning with a sweat-soaked shirt,

Wondering what it would be like if I had been Richard DeWert.

A hardened smile that echoed tears of pain,

A mother's neglect at leaving her child in the rain.

He went willingly with visions of heroism and pride,

To become a Hospital Corpsman in our Nations' fight.

With hopes of the future, to be a doctor someday,

A harsh taste of combat and the dreams fade away.

It was early April with Dog 2/7,

No angels of mercy were looking down from heaven.

A bitter long trek to the 38th parallel,

When they took enemy fire and his Marines began to yell.

"Everybody down, we're in for a fight."

the smell of fear and death took them into the night.

On patrol the next morning as a thick fog rolled in,

The eerie silence of what was to begin.

Suddenly the fog lifted as quickly as it came,

The platoon's being cut down by bullets in vain.

Cries for "Doc" were all that he heard,

Marines gasping for air as they said their last word.

"Don't go out there Doc, wait until it's time,"

a reply was met with, "You do your job, I'll do mine."

No time for thinking, they're bleeding fast,

He pulled his first Marine to safety as he felt the first blast.

His leg burning, a sharp pain indeed,

Ignored for the comfort of his Marines in need.

Dodging through bullets, a daring second trip,

He carried the injured from the enemy's tight grip.

Undaunted by his own condition, his only thought of saving lives,

Dashing automatic fire for a third grueling time.

Another sharp blast of enemy fire,

Piercing pain to his shoulder and he's beginning to tire.

Persistent in his commitment of saving these men,

Out for a fourth time to meet the enemy again.

Assuring his Marines it was going to be alright,

Machine gun fire rendered his mortal plight.

As he lay over the Marine he was to save,

A thousand angels laid feathers at his blood-soaked grave.

As for the men who witnessed such courage and compassion,

They were inspired to move quickly against the enemy's action.

Some say it was Doc, who saved them all,

His selfless sacrifice in answering the call.

I woke up this morning with a calm and grace,

As I looked in the mirror and saw my face.

I realized a few things about my wondering and dismay,

About the legacy Richard DeWert has left us today.

The Hospital Corps can forever stand tall,

For this young man, so fragile, gallantly gave his all.

The Medal of Honor is what they gave,

His selfless deeds so proud and brave.

Long may you rest, our brother DeWert,

No longer to bear the pain of those that are hurt.

Chapter 8
Revenge of a Sort for Hoengsong

If You Find a Prisoner, Bring Him Back

We learned on April 9, 1951, that we were going to raid the Chinese positions on Objective 491, a hill across the valley from our position with an elevation of about fifteen hundred feet. We searched through our Marine Corps guidebooks for the definition of "raid." It was all combat to us.

Our leaders told us that we were going to attack this position, hold it for a certain time, and then vacate it and go back to our lines. We were also to bring back prisoners, if possible, because S2 (Intelligence) wanted some for questioning. We were told that we were going to have tanks, forward observers from artillery, mortars, and air support to back us up.

Raid? It sounded like a full-scale offensive to us. Not quite: our operation was labeled a company raid (Dog/7). With all that support, we felt we could take Moscow.

This was the first time we had done a raid. To take a position and not defend it was new to us. It was easier at times to take an enemy objective and not defend it, because when defending an objective the enemy knew our strengths, knew when we might not be dug in defensively or might be short of ammo, and knew if we might have suffered casualties. They had their reserve forces rested and ready.

Thanks, but No Tanks?

At daybreak we started down the hill from our position and met tanks at the start of the valley. The valley included a small stream or two, which we waded across alongside the tanks, which didn't make the water any drier. But they sure attracted attention.

Tank support was a mixed blessing. They gave great fire support, but they also drew enemy fire. Chinese mortar rounds started to drop among the tanks and the infantry walking alongside. The tankers buttoned up; we couldn't. They were protected by all the armor that tanks are made of, but the infantry marines were only protected by their thin cotton utility jackets.

We left the tanks in the valley and started up Objective 491, but we would utilize their help as the "raid" continued. When they saw our supporting arms, the Chinese were in shock. Some of them left their foxholes and started to run. We immediately noticed something familiar about their uniforms.

A lot of the Chinese soldiers were wearing American-style field jackets that had US Army Second Division patches on them. That sealed their fates. We took the opportunity to gain a small measure of retribution for the "Massacre at Hoengsong."

Later I wrote to my brother, who was a captain in the army at that time, and told him that we had a field day. I told him that we took two mountaintops and killed many Chinese. "They ran into us, and it was like shooting at shapes that were targets and not people. It was exciting," I told him. I also noted, "The Chinese don't die as hard as they used to. I truly believe they have a real fear of marines. The prisoners say this when questioned." Now, when I read that old letter, the things I said sound primitive. But that was the mind-set of young gung ho marines at that time.

We Lose Sergeant Robert Vincent Damon

When the company machine gunners who were giving us covering fire got low on ammo, Chuck Curley volunteered to run down the hill to the tanks in the valley and ask for .30-caliber machine-gun ammo. He and Curtis Mason raced down to the lead tank and placed their request. The tankers readily gave them four cans of ammo.

The pair "fast-tracked" it back up the hill to their machine guns and continued to give covering fire support. Their quick thinking was well-received by the rest of us—especially those among us who appreciated the value of machine gun support.

After the fighting, Captain Mackin told his wife, Mary, in a letter about twenty men being wounded and one man killed, who he said was a great marine. That "great marine" was Sergeant Robert Damon, a World War II marine and Bronze Star recipient who was recalled to active duty for the Korean War. His death struck us platoon members hard, especially those who were near him when he died.

Sergeant Damon was the most caring and righteous marine I ever met. We all called him "Mother Damon" because he worried about all the young marines in our company. He helped the exhausted young marine carry his pack. Damon always seemed to have a swallow of water left in his canteen to give to a marine who was dying of thirst. Somehow, he managed to get the wounded down the hill in the dark and had a knack for saying the right words to a troubled marine.

Sergeant Robert Damon was killed while charging an enemy bunker. He was carrying a 1903 Springfield bolt-action sniper rifle with a ten-power scope, but that was not an assault rifle. It was for sniping, and it was hard to load, which made it less than an ideal weapon for the type of fighting we were doing on Hill 491. He used his pistol instead.

For the attack on the bunker, he took out his pistol and emptied it into the aperture of the enemy bunker. The Chinese shot back and killed him. He received a Silver Star posthumously for his heroic actions.

Silver Star Citation for Damon

> For conspicuous gallantry and intrepidity in action against the enemy while serving with a Marine infantry company in Korea on 10 April 1951. Serving as a guide of a rifle platoon, Sergeant Damon was moving with a squad in the platoon attack of a strongly defended enemy hill position when the unit was subjected to intense and accurate enemy automatic weapons fire from an enemy bunker, and was temporarily unable to advance. Realizing that the successful accomplishment of the platoon's mission depended on the rapid advance of the squad, he fearlessly and with complete disregard for his personal safety charged forward through the heavy enemy fire in a furious assault of the position. When he had expended all his rifle ammunition, he continued forward, courageously firing his pistol

> into the aperture of the bunker until he fell mortally wounded, gallantly giving his life for his country. His great personal bravery and outstanding devotion to duty so inspired his comrades that they swept forward and rapidly secured the objective. Sergeant Damon's heroic actions were in keeping with the highest traditions of the United States Naval Service.

Perry Dickey Remembers

Now a retired lawyer, Perry J. Dickey was a member of the Second Platoon, Dog/7, on the night that Sergeant Damon was killed in action. Damon was his squad leader when they attacked the bunker together that night. He wrote the following account of the events that happened before, during, and after Damon's death:

> On April 10, 1951, Dog Company was on what I believed to be a combat patrol to locate and engage the enemy and to establish a major point of resistance rather than a rearguard action to delay our advance. We had made contact and were receiving small arm and machine gun fire from our right. Rounds were cracking in all directions and one round ricocheted off a small tree branch in front of my head, showering my face and eyes with bark and debris. Then it struck the man to my right, PFC Jose Flores, in the face.

At that time Sergeant Robert Damon came to my left and tapped me on the shoulder, indicating for me to follow him. Sergeant Damon and I started moving to our left and up the hill toward the enemy. We progressed forward about a hundred or more yards, and I think out of sight of other company members. I was several yards behind Sergeant Damon when he shouted, "Shoot 'em!!"

Sergeant Damon had an 03 Springfield sniper rifle with a scope mounted over the receiver. The rifle could hold six rounds, but each round had to be loaded separately into the magazine, and he wanted to withhold firing his rifle. Sergeant Damon had spotted a rifle barrel in the bushes about two yards in front of him when he yelled, "Shoot 'em!" I also saw the rifle and fired into the bush.

At this time another enemy with his rifle aimed at me appeared about ten feet in front of me but slightly to the right side. I fired at him, but my M-1 rifle went click and did not fire. Instantly, I started dropping to the ground and used my left hand to slide the bolt back to clear and load another round into my rifle. I fired again with the rifle at my hip and in a crouched position, and I was fortunate to hit the enemy with a shot between his eyes that blew out the top of his head.

Now hand grenades started to fall and explode all around me. I made a dive for cover, as there was a tree uphill and a small rock protruding from the ground. When I hit the ground I saw three hand grenades tied together and just beyond my reach a few feet uphill and to the right side of my head. I turned my head away from the grenades as they exploded. I was surprised at being alive after they exploded.

I looked to my left and saw Sergeant Damon standing on top of a bunker and firing a .38 revolver into the entrance. He fired several rounds, and then I think there was more than one shot, possibly a volley, from the bunker, and Sergeant Damon was fatally shot in the chest at a range of a few feet. The revolver rotated on his trigger finger and dropped into the bunker. He staggered a step or two toward me and fell face down and with his head downhill. There was a tree stump about a foot high, and Sergeant Damon fell with his chest on the stump, an arm on each side and with his head drooping but not touching the ground. He uttered a small gasp; a large volume of blood gushed from his mouth, and he was dead.

Sergeant Damon's body was about six feet from me and between me and the bunker entrance, which was about ten feet away. I was in a blind spot for the bunker and not within the line of fire. The enemy apparently let Sergeant Damon and me progress without firing to avoid giving away their position. I had two hand grenades. I missed with the first grenade by throwing it over and past the bunker entrance. The second grenade went right into the entrance but was promptly thrown back at me and exploded downhill.

My position was known to the enemy within the bunker, but they were afraid to stand up and fire at me. They did hold a rifle up on the outside of the entrance and fire blindly in my direction. I would return fire, attempting to hit the exposed hands and arms. The malfunction of my rifle now became a benefit, as it did not eject the clip after firing the last round, so I was able to quietly reload. I did not intend to storm the bunker with my single-fire rifle, but I held the enemy off and contemplated possible action.

My concern was that the company was on a combat patrol and probably would withdraw after establishing the main line of resistance. I thought Sergeant Damon and I might not be missed until after the company had withdrawn. Sergeant Damon and I had gone forward in the heat of combat without notice to others.

I was determined not to be taken prisoner, and I believed the best course of action was to hold out until dark and try to return to the company position. After an unknown period of time, I looked downhill and saw a face staring up at me. It was Private Raymond McCallum, who was a replacement that joined our unit a few days earlier.

McCallum had been concerned about his conduct when first exposed to combat, and I had advised him to follow me, do what he had been trained to do, and that he would be okay. McCallum complied with that advice and now was in the line of fire of the bunker about fifty yards downhill.

I motioned for him to withdraw and return with help. He understood and disappeared. Sometime later PFC Gus Felt came inching up from below and to my right. Gus had grenades and was better than I in using them. Gus pulled the pin, let the spoon fly, held the grenade with a grin as I squirmed, and he threw the grenade, which went into the bunker entrance and exploded immediately.

Gus and I continued up the hill, where we encountered more enemy, who were in disarray. Gus and I proceeded to fire at will upon the enemy, who were about one hundred yards away and not returning fire. It was more like target practice than combat.

Gradually other men arrived, and after some time we withdrew and started down the hill. Sergeant Damon's body was removed before I returned to the location. I did help another wounded Marine from our platoon down the hill. He was a squad leader, and I do not remember his name. His left leg was injured, and he was unable to walk. After getting him down the hill, I kept his rifle and destroyed my defective rifle. At that time I became the squad leader to replace Sergeant Damon, who was posthumously awarded a Silver Star and Purple Heart.

Brendan O'Donnell's Account

Second Lieutenant Brendan O'Donnell was patrol leader during the raid on April 10, 1951. He wrote:

> My recollections may bring additional info. I was the patrol leader that day. This was a Dog Company patrol, and the Second Platoon was the lead platoon.

Damon and Perry were in my line of sight as they moved forward on the enemy. Prior to their move we were held up by mortar, machine gun, and small arms fire. I was in radio contact with Captain Mackin and asked him to make sure the mortar fire was not coming from our 4.2 mortars and requested air support.

Marine/naval support came in quickly with napalm and machine guns and opened the spur we were trying to advance up. Prior to the air strike the mortars had miraculously stopped firing. Then Damon and Perry went into action.

You have described our mission correctly. We were a company patrol, reinforced with tanks, artillery, mortars, air support, and forward observers. No enemy contact had been made in a week. We were ordered to attack an identified position, capture prisoners, rout them from their position, hold it for a short time, and return before dark. After the air strike we were able to go to the top of Hill 491, which was loaded with abandoned communications equipment and paper files.

The mission was considered successfully completed—made contact with enemy, drove enemy from strategic position, captured military intelligence files, broke up communications networks, captured prisoners, killed and wounded the enemy. My patrol killed twenty-seven, wounded thirty-five, and captured seven enemy troops. We had one KIA and twenty-two WIA.

We counted their dead and wounded and left all for the enemy to handle. Some were badly burned with white phosphorus and in shock, but we had to move down fifteen hundred feet and then climb up to our command perimeter to complete our mission. I was awarded the Silver Star medal for this mission.

I wrote to Damon's wife and family immediately following the action. A few years before the Mystic Reunion, I received a postcard with a picture of four or five men at a high elevation facing an American flag and the Marine Corps flag. They were men from the April 1951 patrol, along with Bob Mommsen, Damon's son. The flags were stuck in the ground on Hill 491 where Sergeant Damon fell fifty-two years earlier. Bob thanked me for my letter to his family.

Brendan O'Donnell's Silver Star Citation

> For conspicuous gallantry and intrepidity as a Rifle Platoon Commander of Company D, Second Battalion, Seventh Marines, First Marine Division (Reinforced), in action against enemy aggressor forces in Korea on 10 April 1951. Assigned the mission of leading the company assault on a strongly defended enemy hill position to learn the enemy's disposition in the area and to capture prisoners, Second Lieutenant O'DONNELL skillfully maneuvered his platoon up the steep slope and effectively coordinated his advance with supporting arms, surprising the enemy and aiding his platoon in killing 27, wounding 35 and capturing 7 of the enemy. Although exposed at all times to withering hostile automatic weapons fire from

adjacent hills, he succeeded in organizing the defense of the position. With his unit subjected to an intense mortar barrage, causing numerous casualties and destroying radio communications with his company commander, he led his remaining force forward in the assault on an adjacent ridge to relieve pressure on another element of the company which was pinned down by hostile fire. Fearlessly exposing himself to a withering cross fire of enemy automatic weapons, he led his men in a furious assault on the ridge, routing the enemy and permitting the other friendly elements to advance. By his inspiring leadership, aggressive fighting spirit and courageous initiative, Second Lieutenant O'DONNELL contributed materially to the success of the company and upheld the highest traditions of the United States Naval Service.

Robert Damon's Obituary

Robert Vincent Damon was born March 10, 1922, in Seattle, Washington. He completed his first ten years of school work in Walla Walla, Washington, and then moved with his parents, Professor and Mrs. V. L. Damon, to Colville, Washington, where he finished high school. Professor Damon was a minister as well as a college professor. Robert V. Damon graduated with an AB degree from Seattle Pacific College, and then continued with graduate work at the University of Washington. He had almost completed his work for his Master's Degree when he was again called to go with the Marines to Korea.

He was in defense work at Pearl Harbor, Hawaii, when the attack was made on December 7, 1941. After returning to Seattle the following summer, he enlisted in the Marines, although he had been granted an exemption because of his plans for entering the ministry.

On December 4, 1943, he was united in marriage to Charlotte H. Anderson of Cove, Washington, in San Diego, California. He left in about three weeks for Honolulu. He was in the battles of both Saipan and Tinian, then returned to Saipan until after the close of the war when he was sent to Japan with the occupation forces for a few weeks. He returned to the United States in January 1946, and he and his wife made their home in Seattle, Washington.

A fellow Marine who returned to his home in Walla Walla, Washington, just a few weeks ago said when he learned of Robert's death, "It's not right; he was always the good one of the bunch. He never said any bad words; he was so clean living and good." He also said he was easy with the men under him and they liked him so well.

In a letter to personal friends he recently stated: "I participated in the two weeks campaign which pushed the enemy from Hoengsong to the high ground beyond Hoengch'on. Only the grace of God made it possible for me to carry out my duties. It is evident that I still have work to do or would not have been passed over (or around) by the enemy fire."

Robert leaves to mourn his going, his wife Charlotte, son, Robert Vincent II, age 3 1/2, Kathleen Ann, age 8 months, his father and mother, Mr. and Mrs. V.L. Damon, an older sister, Mrs. Margaret Zucher of Pasadena, California, two brothers, William Burns of Walla Walla, Washington, and Albert M. of Sterling, also a host of relatives and friends.

More Information on Robert Damon

Robert V. Damon met his wife, Charlotte, at Seattle Pacific College. He was getting a master's degree at the University of West Seattle and was 99 percent complete with his studies when he was recalled to active duty in the Marine Corps after the outbreak of the Korean War.

Sergeant Damon's widow married Laddie Mommsen in 1959. Mr. Mommsen formerly served in the army in Africa and Italy during World War II. He adopted Robert's children, and their names were changed to Robert and Kathleen Mommsen. Robert now lives in Ketchikan, Alaska, where he was at one time a bush pilot and now works on an inland ship. Kathleen Damon was born in August 1950, one month after her father left for the Korean War. She was a baby when Sergeant Damon was killed in action in Korea. Kathleen Pugerude now lives in Forest Grove, Oregon. Mr. and Mrs. Laddie Mommsen live in Lynnwood, Washington.

A Belated—and Sad—Mail Call

After we secured Hill 491, we started to go through the pockets of the dead Chinese that were wearing army field jackets. We retrieved the mail and billfolds that they had taken from army soldiers killed at Hoengsong. Reading this mail later made us happy that we did what we did to get it back.

We left Hill 491 at 4:00 p.m. with seven prisoners. None of them were wearing army field jackets.

Chapter 9
The Impossible Is Possible

Reserved—but Not Shy

Lealon Wimpee became our new platoon leader on April 7, 1951. Less than a month later this great officer and the members of D-2-7 were once again in harm's way.

On April 22, 1951, we walked down from our hill position and finally returned to reserve after thirty-seven days on line. It was about 10:00 a.m., and we desperately needed rest. We were exhausted from constant patrols, combat, and no rest. We needed about twenty hours of sleep. We also were in need of a change of clothing. Mountain warfare wore out our clothes. The only pockets that were not torn were our breast pockets.

In a perfect world, ten days on line and five days in reserve is the norm. We asked Captain Mackin why we were kept on line so long without rest. He said it was because we didn't have enough continuous time with our regiment. Because they kept moving us from the First Marine Division to the First Cavalry Division and then back to the First Marine

Division, we didn't build up any credits with any one unit. I didn't quite understand this, but I did understand that we desperately needed rest and a bath.

Saddle Up

We started to unpack and get out our sleeping bags when we were told to saddle up because we were moving back on line to plug a gap on our flanks. The Chinese had destroyed an ROK division near Hwachon, and we had to stop them or our main line would collapse. This was the closest we ever got to mutiny. But Captain Mackin was a man who could get the guys going and do the impossible. With no rest, we endured a fast-paced, fifteen-mile hike over mountains with a full pack.

We saw helicopters flying overhead—lots of them. It was the First Battalion Seventh Marines flying to war. It was the first time ever that helicopters were used to transport troops to a combat zone.

It started to rain, and the showers continued as we hiked. As darkness set in, the showers became a full-fledged rainstorm. We were walking up the mountainside slipping and sliding when someone slipped and let out an obscenity. He said that he had fallen on a stob.

Someone asked what a stob was, and then we all started laughing. One marine said, "You baby. You ought to be home with your mother."

Then a bunch of others joined in and said they ought to be home with their mothers too. In all of this misery, this was funny. But the fun didn't last long.

Two Enemies, Same Objective

After a while we could hear the Chinese talking close to us.

They were hiking parallel to us, heading for the same high ground as us. It was bizarre—the rainstorm, the Chinese going in the same direction in the dark, and them yelling at us from time to time.

When dawn arrived, the sun came up in a big orange ball. The rain had stopped, and we were on the mountaintop. The mountain was hollowed out to a big room with a deep trench line all around it. About fifty yards below us was another trench line that circled around the mountain. It was full of Chinese troops. We had beaten them up the mountain in the rain and the dark. Thank you, Captain Mackin!

From the top of Hill 722 (about twenty-three hundred feet high), we could see practically forever in the valley where marine and army vehicles, hub to hub, relied on us for protection. By beating the Chinese to the high ground in the rain and dark, Captain Mackin kept the Chinese from calling artillery and mortar fire on the troops in the valley. It also meant that we did not have to fight to get the high ground. He who controls the high ground wins! A lot of marines to this day are enjoying their grandchildren and the rest of their lives thanks to Captain Alvin Mackin.

Later, I asked Captain Mackin how he found this old commie defensive position with the old Japanese maps. Drawn circa 1905, those old maps were often erroneous, with mountaintops missing or out of place. Captain Mackin just shrugged his shoulders and said, "I just guessed and got lucky." How he could read the maps in the dark and rain is another story.

The Chinese troops in the trench line below us were in a vulnerable spot. The trench was deep and had a roof over a large part of it. In the center of the trench, there was a roof next to the mountainside that went almost straight down the rest of the trench, covering possible approaches.

I was a squad leader; Captain Mackin told me that we were going to take the trench line below at about 10:00 a.m. to protect Fox Company, which would be passing through about that time. After taking the trench we were to follow Fox Company down the valley and act as rear guard.

Lieutenant Wimpee was in radio contact with Fox Company. He told Captain Mackin that Fox Company was ahead of schedule, and we would have to take the trench now! He also told me that he was going to lead the squad in the assault. We climbed out of our trench and started to walk toward the Chinese trench. Walking over that open ground toward an enemy position felt a little tingly.

As we got closer, Lieutenant Wimpee threw a grenade to the right trench, toward the roof. The grenade was thrown back immediately; it exploded behind some rocks. Lieutenant Wimpee pulled the pin on a second grenade, waited a few seconds, and threw it into the same place. When it detonated, he and the marines following him jumped into the right side of the trench. I took a fire team and jumped in the left side.

The Chinese, who were trying to get away from Lieutenant Wimpee and his marines, ran right into us. It was a wild few moments. The older World War II marines used to tell us, "You haven't killed the enemy unless you get that dying quiver." I could now relate to that.

Wimpee Teaches Marines the Danger of Being Wimpy

As we walked through the trench and under the roof toward Lieutenant Wimpee, we saw wounded and dead Chinese soldiers. Lieutenant Wimpee grabbed hold of one marine by the jacket, shoved him against the wall, and started yelling at him, "When they quit, you quit. Hear me?!"

He took the marine's rifle away, gave it to a fellow marine, and said, "Hold this rifle, and do not give it back to him until I tell you to!"

Another bunker was a little way down the trail. Lieutenant Wimpee ran ahead of us and threw a grenade into it. When we checked the bunker, two dead Chinese were inside.

Once we had been surrounded; now the trail to the valley was clear. However, there were Chinese on our flanks firing at extreme rifle distances from the mountaintops on both sides of us.

We took two prisoners onto the bunker rooftop and lit cigarettes for them for all to see. When the firing toward us stopped, we put bandages on their heads. (They had leg wounds.) We also put bandages on their arms.

I said that we had better stop with the bandages, as our prisoners were beginning to look like mummies. This was a PR trick that worked. We took our prisoners and followed Fox Company down the hill with no more harassing fire from our flanks.

Adrenaline Rush

Participants in competitive sports can relate to the words "adrenaline rush." The human body produces a rush of adrenaline during times of high emotion or high excitement. While athletes get this rush in competition, soldiers experience it during combat.

For those in a fight for life, this rush is a psychological condition that arises in response to terrifying or traumatic events. It occurs in that moment in time when combatants get an extra burst of energy while fighting for their life against an enemy who is out to kill them.

Later, I asked Lieutenant Wimpee how he could turn off all the adrenaline rush of combat so quickly. He said, "When they quit, we quit. We are marines, not murderers."

I never forgot that. I said to myself, "I am glad he did not see us when we were in combat at the other end of the trench." You do not want to do things in combat that you may be ashamed of later.

Silver Star Forty-Nine Years Later

On December 7, 1998, I wrote to Colonel Alvin F. Mackin (USMC Ret.), requesting that he put Lee Wimpee up for a citation. He agreed to do so if I would write up the action and send it to him. He signed it and sent it up the line.

My letter to Colonel Mackin read:

> As I remember, the following events took place April 23, 1951, while serving with D-2-7 in Korea as a fire team leader. The 7th Marines were just returning to the rest area as Division reserve was recalled back on line to stop a Chinese Communist breakthrough on our flank.
>
> It was midmorning, and we started toward the break to stop the Chinese from overrunning the UN positions. We walked all that day and into the night at a fast and exhausting pace.
>
> I recall walking into a very heavy thunderstorm. We were racing for the high ground to reach a strategic position ahead of the Chinese. We were in conflict

with enemy forces most of the night. They were following us up the hill.

Before daybreak the rain stopped. We were on top of a hill that was a prewar defensive position, with dugout rooms and trenches around the top. In the valley below we could see UN vehicles and personnel gathering to withdraw to a new line of defense. We had beaten the Chinese to the high ground. I think this saved the UN forces in the valley from being shelled by Chinese artillery. Dog Company was under your command.

The scenario as I remember was like this. Dog Company was on top of the hill; Chinese forces were in old prewar trenches just below Dog Company, and UN forces were in the valley. Dog Company was completely surrounded by the enemy. Dog Company was to act as rear guard for the UN forces in the valley. To do this Dog Company had to break through enemy defenses in bunkers and trenches below our position.

I was in the point to engage the enemy. Lt. Lealon Wimpee, third platoon leader, advanced ahead of the point, took charge of the attacking Marines, and led them toward enemy positions. Lt. Wimpee threw a grenade into the enemy trenches. The grenade was thrown back by the Chinese and exploded behind some rocks.

Lt. Wimpee threw another grenade that went off where the trench went into the enemy bunker. Lt. Wimpee then charged the bunker with other Marines behind him, killing many of the enemy and taking prisoners. This allowed Dog Company to move safely down the hill to provide a rear guard to the UN forces in the valley, thus allowing friendly forces to make a strategic withdrawal.

It is my understanding that you had recommended Lt. Wimpee for a Silver Star or a Navy Cross. Somehow this recommendation was lost. I hope this letter helps in getting Lealon Wimpee the long-overdue citation that he justly earned. Lt. Wimpee is held in high regard by all those who served with him. We would be honored if you would resubmit your former recommendation for an award for this worthy Marine.

If I can be of any more help in achieving this award for Lealon Wimpee, please contact me.

Semper Fidelis, Fred Frankville

Humility as well as bravery were common traits of this great officer. I take pride in the fact that I was instrumental in getting Lieutenant Wimpee the Silver Star medal forty-nine years after his heroic actions on Hill 722.

Lieutenant Wimpee's Silver Star citation reads:

For conspicuous gallantry and intrepidity in action while serving with Dog Company, 2nd Battalion, 7th Marines east of Hill 722 in the Republic of Korea on 23 April 1951. Serving as rear guard for the battalion, Second Lieutenant WIMPEE accurately assessed the enemy preparing to ambush the withdrawing Fox Company. Seeing the gravity of the situation, he led a squad down the hill to eliminate the threat. After an exchange of grenade throwing, Second Lieutenant WIMPEE leaped into the trench and bunker with the other Marines following; the enemy position was taken with numerous Chinese killed and several prisoners taken. Second Lieutenant WIMPEE then continued the attack to the next Chinese position, throwing grenades and firing into the trench and bunker, clearing all resistance. By his outstanding bravery, inspiring initiative, and courageous devotion to duty, Second Lieutenant WIMPEE saved the lives of fellow Marines; thereby reflecting great credit upon himself and upholding the highest traditions of the Marine Corps and the United States Naval Service.

Chapter 10
Late Spring Springs

Letting the Air Out of Our Defenses

In the late part of spring 1951 we were issued rubber air mattresses. A simple thing like an air mattress was a great improvement over lying on the bare ground or the pine branches we had been using to insulate us from the cold ground. The only problems with using the air mattresses were that they raised us up about four or five inches higher in our foxholes and they added several pounds to the weight of equipment we carried.

One night while we were in our foxholes enjoying the comfort of our new air mattresses, we detected the faint odor of garlic. The Chinese and North Koreans ate garlic like popcorn. So, if they were close and the wind was in the right direction, we could smell them before we could see them.

All up and down the line we could hear the air being let out of the air mattresses. It was a Chinese probing attack testing our defenses at several points, hoping to draw automatic weapons fire so that they could detect the locations of our machine guns and then call mortar fire on the guns. This was a tactic the enemy used that usually preceded an all-out attack. Marines were familiar with this tactic and maintained fire discipline until the time of the actual assault.

Whistling on the Phone

We also had an outpost in front of each platoon, about fifty yards out more or less, depending on the terrain. The outpost had a sound power phone linked up with each platoon and the company command center. On this particular night, outpost three said there was an enemy patrol around their position.

Someone replied, "Shoot them."

The marines at the outpost said, "No. There are too many of them." Worse, the Chinese were between the outpost and our lines—which meant the men on the outpost could not return to our lines. That was when some smart-ass started whistling on the phone.

The outpost crew pulled the wires off the phone so the enemy patrol could not hear the whistling. At daybreak, the outpost marines returned to the lines ready to fight. They wanted to know who the son of a bitch was who was whistling into the phone. All the time looking at us. We all claimed innocence. In retrospect, those marines had a right to bitch. That whistling on the phone could literally have led them to whistling not past, but into, the graveyard. Sometimes gallows humor went a little too far in potentially dangerous situations.

"Low-Tech" Job

Being a marine rifleman was a "low-tech" job. If you could throw rocks, you could do what I did. From the time the Twenty-First Engineer Battalion was activated in Moline in

August 1950 until December 23, 1951, I did not get a day off. That was about sixteen months of duty with no day off. There was no such thing as rest and recuperation (R & R) during those months. Instead, we lived in a Stone Age environment. Troops got dysentery and—can you believe it?—worms.

The Koreans used human waste to fertilize their fields. We drank out of rivers and streams that had run off from the fields. We carried Halazone tablets that we put in our canteens fifteen minutes before drinking from them. (Halazone was a white, crystalline powder with a strong taste and smell of chlorine. Usually it was used in tablet form to disinfect small quantities of drinking water.)

The chlorine-based tablets were supposed to sterilize the water, but I don't think the Halazone actually worked in this environment. I remember that Captain Mackin was evacuated to the hospital ship USS *Haven* for worm treatment. On August 5, 1951, he wrote the following to his wife:

> Today was a hot, sticky day which followed a terrific rain we had last night. For the past ten days or so my stomach has been out of whack—probably a bug of some sorts—or worms. You'd be surprised at some of the worm cases we do have. Many boys with nausea have vomited worms almost a foot long!
>
> Getting back to the main subject: I decided to go to sickbay. I got paregoric, amphogel(?) pills, and aurenycin. It's beginning to fix me up now—at least my cramps have stopped. (Hoagie Carmichael just sang "Lime House Blues.")

He then wrote to his wife, Mary, on August 16, 1951, about the treatment he took for his affliction. His letter said:

My Darling, it's worms! (I sound like a proud father announcing a blessed event. If I do it's because it's a relief to know now that my troubles aren't of a more serious degree.) The doc informed me of my affliction yesterday and at noon my deworming treatment commenced.

Most important it meant fasting for 24 hours; therefore, I didn't eat from noon yesterday until noon today. During that time I took (under duress) three doses of Epson salts and many, many pills. Starting at midnight and throughout the day I "shot the works."

Man o' man, I've worn a path from my stateroom to the head. I probably look like a man making a mad dash for a train at the station. It would be an unfortunate man who blocked my travel. Right now I feel like a toilet that's been flushed with Babo Cleanser.

I should be out of here and on my way back to regiment within a few days. This ship leaves for Japan on about the 23rd. If I'd had hepatitis I would certainly have been a passenger to Japan and thence to the States. Oh me, which is worse?

All I've done these days is lounge around in my pajamas and bathrobe, take morning and afternoon naps, and watch the evening movies. When I'm in the sack I listen to the radio by means of a set of bedside earphones which come with every bed. What a life! What did Sherman say? Oh, yes. "War is hell!!"

It just occurred to me that this is the first time I've slept indoors since I've been out here. To compensate

> for the great fresh air of the outdoors we have air conditioning, so it's not so bad.
>
> Seriously though. I know this life is going to get on my nerves soon. There's only one thing could change the monotony of all this, and that's to go home! If only there was some set date toward which I could count days and weeks it would mean something to look forward to. As it stands now, however, it's only a guess.

The troops were lined up every month or so, and we passed a gallon jug around that held some junk called Paregoric. We each had to take two swallows. Paregoric is an opium-derived product used to treat diarrhea.

Who Owns the Ford Dealership Here in Korea?

During the first week of May we were patrolling in front of Dog Company positions and beyond when we saw a huge pile of evergreen trees. It looked like a Christmas tree dump. While we were walking by a pile of trees, I saw what looked like a bumper and a headlight. I pulled the trees aside. Lo and behold, I saw a Russian jeep with a truck next to it. Since we were in a supposed "police action," we decided to act like traffic cops.

When we lifted the hood up on the jeep, it looked like a Model A Ford. I had a Model A at home. This was an exact copy, with a four-wheel drive and a Russian body. It had a T distributor, an updraft carburetor, and a flathead four-cylinder engine. The muffler and tailpipe were from a Model A Ford. I thought to myself that I would love to drive it.

I understand that Henry Ford sent Ford tooling to Russian in the midthirties. The truck next to it was a copy of a 1941

Chevrolet one-and-a-half-ton truck. It may have been a Lend-Lease American truck sent to Russia during World War II.

After we returned from our patrol, the guys were riding around in the truck. Someone had hotwired the truck and taken it for a ride with a load of marines in back. They also captured a prisoner who was glad to come out of hiding.

For one afternoon Dog/7 had its own motor pool. Captain Mackin was not comfortable with the marines riding around the perimeter in a Russian truck, so he took the truck and other vehicles and gave them to the regimental motor pool.

Task Force Zebra

Task Force Zebra began May 18, 1951. The memoirs of army surgeon Captain Eric Larsen provide details about this task force. He wrote:

> In May 1951 I was assigned to Task Force Zebra, which was comprised of the 23rd Regimental Combat Team, plus additional special units. ... We moved to the eastern sector of the 38th parallel to a town called Chaun-ni near Hill 1051. This narrative is about a great battle I witnessed and participated in which erupted on May 18, 1951.
>
> On the night of May 16, the Chinese began making contact in our area. On the same night, South Korean forces began a disorderly withdrawal ... in spite of orders to remain and fight. I personally witnessed their troops fleeing past my unit without weapons while our officers encouraged them to stop. The following day, May 18, a Chinese patrol got to our area (about 2 a.m.), killing two men and wounding eight others outside my aid tent. They were armed

> with burp guns (shoulder-fired machine guns), which caused gruesome injuries. I saw them swarm like ants down the hills toward our position. Many Chinese were killed at my aid site.
>
> Task Force Zebra was completely cut off from the rest of the UN forces as the only road out was in enemy hands. As relief was not to be forthcoming, it was decided that we would try and run the roadblock with two tank escorts in the point. My jeep with two litters was to follow the tanks. This convoy would consist of several hundred vehicles in which 117 were trucks and jeeps and 76 were trailers. This convoy, loaded with the wounded and soldiers, was doomed to grief.
>
> The lead tank hit a mine about a quarter mile down the road, and was pushed aside by the other tank, which was also soon disabled as well as my jeep, which was blown off the road and into a ditch. In the confusion of the dust and the explosions, I stumbled out of the jeep and found a crater on the right side of the road and witnessed the tankers being killed as they were in the process of trying to escape the tanks.
>
> I also saw Chinese soldiers with burp guns alongside of the roads, shooting at our troops in the trucks and alongside of the trucks. This sight was horrible and depressing. I shall never forget it.

According to his memoirs, Captain Larsen was next to a river. He dove into the river and ran, waded, and swam across the river with bullets splashing the water near him. He made it to the other side and was picked up by a retreating tank. Captain Larsen lived to write his memories and to revisit Korea September 10–17, 2003.

Dog/7 Marines was the first unit to find this massacre alongside the road near Chaun-ni on May 22, 1951. I have seen a list of over three hundred soldiers who were killed on May 18, 1951, in Chaun-ni. To me, this shows that the Americans were bunched up with no room to maneuver and defend themselves. The same thing happened north of Hoengsong, where Dog/7 marines found mostly Second Division troops massacred alongside of Road 24.

This carnage was blamed on South Korean forces who failed to protect the Americans. The sad part is, the army top brass did not learn this lesson from what happened at Hoengsong on February 12–14, 1951. The carnage was repeated at Chaun-ni on May 18, 1951, where South Korean forces who were supposed to defend the Americans just ran away. Where was the outrage for this failure of command?

Chapter 11
I Thanked the Lord That I Was a Marine

Another Massacre

On May 22 or 23 we walked to an area near Chaun-ni. We were told that the Twenty-Third RCT of the army's Second Division forces had been overrun and massacred by Chinese army forces. When we reached the area where the massacre occurred, we could see trucks and jeeps alongside the road. Some of the vehicles still contained bodies; it seemed like some of them were in trucks that had been torched. The Twenty-Third RCT, part of the US Army Second Division, was cut off when they attempted to escape by truck down a road controlled by the Chinese.

Perry Dickey Remembers

Former member of Second Platoon, Dog/7, Perry Dickey, still has memories of the scene to this day. He had this to say about the burnt carnage:

> My memory of Massacre Valley is somewhat dim, but I do recall that in May 1951 we passed through a valley with US Army vehicles that burned and some of them still occupied with the bodies of US Army personnel. My only vivid memory is a US Army six-by with about six bodies. One of them was sitting on the bench seat inside of the truck in a natural position, except the body appeared to be charcoaled. The temperature was warm, but I do not remember any odor of decaying bodies or any other evidence to show when the event occurred or the passage of time. We continued to move out and did not linger to inspect the bodies or any equipment.

Remember, in early March 1951 we had found hundreds of Second Division troops massacred alongside their trucks north of Hoengsong. When I saw stuff like that, I thanked the Lord that I was a marine. We had been on line for sixty-two days. We were dressed in rags, ate canned junk, and had dysentery, worms, and who knows what else. But we were led by the best combat officers in the world. They suffered with us, and they kept us alive.

Death by Truck

If I was going to write a story about the army's Second Division, it would be entitled "Death by Truck." They went on line riding in trucks. They returned from being on line to a rest area by truck. They retreated by truck. Trucks caused traffic jams; traffic jams caused roadblocks; trucks filled with soldiers stopped by roadblocks were called targets. General Ridgway knew this. He told the army to get rid of trucks and have the troops walk the ridgeline like the marines.

Certainly, US Army soldiers would argue that point of

view. In fact, some of them have told me in no uncertain terms that I am wrong. They relied on trucks too much, though. Consider this scenario from October 1950 when the UN troops were pushing the North Koreans back into their own country. (The Chinese had not yet entered the war.)

(Logistics) The advance of the US Eighth Army into North Korea is causing problems. Because of damage done by air strikes, rail transportation is unable to move all of the needed supplies, troops, and equipment. A heavy burden falls on trucks using poor roads for long hauls. In turn this causes many of the trucks to break down, but the spare parts needed are not available.

This problem grows during October as the Eighth Army moves farther north and three-quarters of the Eighth Army's trucks are operating twenty-four hours a day. Trucks are taken away from the Second and Twenty-Fifth Divisions, which are still in South Korea. At times front-line divisions send men back to Pusan by air to drive trucks back, over four hundred miles on bad roads, to their units.

And riding in them was fraught with peril. I have already mentioned two massacres we came across in which being trapped in trucks led to the deaths of numerous American and South Korean troops. But small-scale ambushes were just as lethal.

Consider this event that occurred on October 22, 1950, as described by a US Army lieutenant, Sam Holliday, in his book, *Up and Down Korea*:

> 22 October 1950: In the Chinsan-Kunsan area, south of Taejon, 35th Regt, 25th Div. is conducting anti-

> guerrilla operations against local communists who have controlled this area for many years.
>
> I had planned to take two trucks with soldiers to fill-in two trenches across a road southwest of Chinsan. At the last minute I was asked to do something else, so I sent my most valued NCO, Sgt Gousnell, and my interpreter, Paul, to guide the two trucks. Forty minutes later word came that they had been ambushed. When the rescue force arrives the trucks are burning and only bodies remain. Each body has no shoes and at least two wounds—one always through the back of the head. The body of Paul is found, but the body of Sgt Gousnell is not there.

Incidents like that one explain why marines, for the most part, walked, rather than rode on trucks. And we stayed off the roads and on the high ground whenever possible. As one axiom of military leadership suggests, "He who holds the high road holds the advantage." Of course, such axioms were well above my pay grade, but marines spent a lot of time above the road, which is one of the reasons I am still alive—and glad I was a marine.

And the Chinese and North Koreans did not rely on trucks to any great extent. For one thing, UN air superiority kept them off the roads, especially during the daytime. But they really did not need them. The Chinese and North Koreans traveled light, as Holliday explained.

While firepower superiority (better artillery, tanks, and airplanes) can bring military success, it can be neutralized by camouflage discipline and surprise. The Chinese are well trained in the techniques of concealment and deception.

While trucks give maneuver superiority where there is a good road network, trucks hinder tactical mobility where there are few roads. On mountain trails, tactical maneuver superiority goes to well-conditioned foot soldiers with pack animals. Each Chinese soldier carries enough food and ammunition for five days, so Chinese Communist Forces units are able to move on trails and poor roads without the need of a large supply train.

On October 24–28, 1950, the Chinese were able to defeat the ROK divisions moving toward the Yalu River, since they were able to neutralize the ROK's superior technology and firepower with surprise and tactical maneuver superiority.

Ridgway's View of Trucks

Even General Matthew Ridgway recognized that trucks could be an impediment to US Army operations in Korea at times, due in great part to the roads—or lack thereof.

Some army veterans challenged me to provide supporting evidence to prove that Ridgway wanted US soldiers off trucks and on foot. I did a search but could not find a specific order. I did, however, find an article written by Andrew Salmon titled "Savior of the South," for the January 10, 2010, *Korea Times* that supported my contention.

Salmon wrote:

> Untitled documents held in the National War Memorial of Korea indicate that credit for holding the line in face of the war's biggest attacks must go to General Ridgway. General Ridgway took over from General Walker following the latter's death in December 1950.

> Walker was a protégé of General George S. Patton of WWII fame. Walker's offensive dash in late 1950 contributed to the UN catastrophe in North Korea. In the mountain terrain of North Korea, UN tanks had no room for maneuvers like those conducted in Europe during World War II, when Patton protected his flanks by massive tank maneuvers.
>
> The war in Europe was not won by tactics. It was won by logistics and the flat terrain to maneuver massive armored divisions. In Korea, General Walker left a 60-plus mile gap between his Eighth Army's east flank and X Corps. Walker's tanks were restricted in their maneuvers by the lack of roads and the mountainous countryside.
>
> General Walker must share blame with Generals MacArthur and Almond for the disasters in North Korea. The troops paid the price in blood. (Again, my Army colleagues dissent, but facts are facts.)
>
> Ridgway, a paratrooper, insisted that troops in Korea dismount from vehicles, leave the roads, and dominate high ground. His tactics were more cautious than Walker's, but more successful.

That's proof enough that Ridgway and I thought alike, at least as far as the use of trucks in Korea was concerned.

Beer by Truck

Don't get me wrong. We didn't turn down rides on trucks when the conditions were right. On the other hand, trucks sometimes became bones of contention between soldiers and marines, and they had their own war fighting each other instead of against the Chinese and North Koreans—all in good fun, of course.

In the early summer of 1951, army trucks were going up to the front to pick up the army troops we were relieving. The marines "humped," as we did most of the time, and the army rode their trucks most of the time. Sometimes the empty army trucks stopped and picked us up. At other times they did not. We knew that when the army drivers did not give us a ride it was because their trucks had beer in them for the army troops we were relieving.

One time the trucks on the road next to us were going back to the rest area with soldiers in them drinking beer and enjoying themselves. The convoy stopped; we could see the troops drinking beer and laughing. The truck that stopped next to us had a soldier who offered the marine in front of me a beer. When the marine said, "Thanks," and reached for the beer, the soldier pulled it back and said, "Screw you." (He used another term.)

Matters came to a head quickly. The marine pulled a grenade off his harness and threw it into the truck. (He did not pull the pin.) The soldiers saw the grenade bouncing around in the truck and leaped out of the vehicle. Some were actually hurt when they hit the ground in all positions. The marines then jumped in the truck and 'liberated" their beer.

That was one time that we discovered the benefits of the army's use of trucks.

Chapter 12
Operation Mousetrap

Destroying an Enemy Regiment

General Ridgway conceived Operation Mousetrap as part of the counteroffensive called Operation Killer. Mousetrap started in early May and ended in early June 1951. During this operation, there was a battle in which a few marines and their supporting arms destroyed a Chinese army regiment in one of the fiercest firefights of the war. It took place on May 16–17, 1951. Maybe it should have been named the "Battle of Morae Kagae Pass" to separate the battle from the operation.

The Battle of Morae Kagae Pass

Very little is written about this firefight. In researching Operation Mousetrap, I found the following information about the battle in Volume V, *US Marine Operations in Korea*. This series was produced by the Historical Branch, G/3 Headquarters, US Marine Corps, Washington, DC, in 1962. The reference in Volume V to the battle that took place on May 16–17, 1951, states:

> That night Chinese forces entered the Marine zone in regimental strength where the 5th Marines and the Korean Marines had several company-sized patrol bases well north of the main line of resistance in the left and center sections respectively. To the right, Colonel Nickerson's 7th Marines had Lieutenant Colonel John T. Rooney's 1st Battalion patrolling the Chunchon Road, 2d Battalion (now commanded by Lieutenant Colonel Wilbur F. Meyerhoff, formerly the 3d Battalion, 7th Marines, commanding officer) manning the outpost, and Lieutenant Colonel Bernard T. Kelly's 3d Battalion, 7th Marines, holding Morae Kogae Pass—a vital link on the road leading from the forward edge of the battle area back to the main front line.
>
> Well aware that whoever controlled the pass controlled the road, the Chinese made Morae Kogae a key objective. Under cover of darkness, they carefully slipped in behind the Korean Marines and headed straight for the pass, which they apparently thought was unguarded.

The assault force unexpectedly bumped into the northern sector of the 7th Marines perimeter at about 0300 and a furious fight broke out. Within minutes the 11th Marines built up a wall of fire at the same time the infantrymen initiated their final protective fires. Burning tracer rounds criss-crossed all avenues of approach and exploding shells flashed in the night as Marine artillery pinned the enemy in place from the rear while Marine riflemen knocked them down from the front.

In spite of the curtain of steel surrounding the Marine positions, the quilt-coated enemy closed the position. Amid the fierce hand-to-hand fighting, First Lt. Victory Stoyanow led a counterattack to throw the enemy back out of Company I's lines. The critical battle for the pass did not end until daybreak when the Chinese vainly tried to pull back but were instead caught in the open by Marine artillery, mortars, and some belated air strikes.

The Chinese lost an estimated 530 men. By actual count, they left behind 112 dead, 82 prisoners, and a wealth of abandoned weapons that included recoilless rifles, mortars, machine guns, and even a 76mm antitank gun. Marine losses in this one-sided battle were seven dead and 19 wounded.

The following day, May 18th, the 1st Marine Division performed a very tricky maneuver to readjust defensive dispositions that allowed the U.S. 2d Infantry Division to move east to reinforce its right flank which was bearing the brunt of the new Chinese offensive. The 7th Marines pulled back to the No Name Line to relieve the 1st Marines, which then sidestepped east to take over an area previously held by the U.S. Army's 9th Infantry Regiment and the 5th Marines swung over from the far left flank to relieve the 38th Infantry Regiment on the extreme. By noon on the 19th, all four regiments (1st Korean Marine, 7th Marines, 1st Marines, and 5th Marines) were aligned from left to right on the modified No Name Line as the enemy's offensive lost its momentum.

My Memories of Mousetrap

Okay, that's the big picture. But the troops doing the actual fighting never see the big picture. All they see is what is going on in their immediate vicinity, and all they think about is saving their own lives. Here is what I remember about Mousetrap.

We replaced the Army's Thirty-Second Regiment on line

in mid-May 1951 and then continued to walk into enemy territory with Able Company and some other support units to set a trap for Chinese forces. We walked for several miles, staying in the valley between two mountain ranges, without encountering any opposition.

As I remember it, we dug in with Able Company. A/7 was west and Dog/7 east. We dug end-to-end and formed a slightly curved defensive line. I remember a road passing through our defensive position. A tank was on the road as part of our defense.

After dark, at about 10:00 p.m., a battalion-size Chinese assault force hit our defensive position in a narrow area. This human wave tactic was a traditional Communist tactic, hoping to overwhelm the defense by assaulting a platoon or less with large forces. The Communists were willing to take huge losses while hoping to punch through the lines.

The assault took place west of where I was dug in. The curve of our defense position gave most of us a view of the battle. Illuminating grenades, parachute flares, and tracer bullets lit up the firefight. The Chinese hit our lines where Dog and Able came together, with most of them toward Able Company. The Chinese were trading Chinese bodies for marine bullets.

At daybreak the line in front of the assault was covered with Chinese bodies. I heard there were as many as 750 of them. The bodies were searched for weapons; some S-2 people searched for information, records, maps, etc. Then a rather large bulldozer showed up, dug a large ditch for a mass burial of the dead Chinese, and covered the bodies once they were placed in it. Afterward, it looked like freshly plowed ground with no sign of the carnage that had taken place. We then hiked back to our lines.

After-Action Report

Marines I talked to after the fight said if one of us was hit, another would run up and take his place. The Chinese way of fighting—i.e., concentrating on a small perimeter of contact with large forces—allowed the marines on the flanks to replace the casualties in the narrow combat zone. Weather-wise, it had been a terrible week or so, with cold rain, mud, and misery. We were wet most of the time, and there was a lot of cholera among the native population, which put us at more risk.

Perry Dickey, who was serving in Dog Company at the time we were taking part in Operation Mousetrap, remembers the following about it:

> My memory of Operation Mousetrap is limited to a few outstanding events. I do not recall where we were dug in during the night as related to the location of the main battle. Also, I do not recall any significant activity at our location; however, there may have been some activity that was more or less routine with mortar, artillery, and sporadic small-arms fire.
>
> I do remember a bright and sunny morning when we left our position and advanced to the location of the main battle. It was obvious there had been a major fight, as there were many Chinese bodies along the way.
>
> The number of bodies increased as we advanced to the area that was the center of the activity. There were hundreds of bodies, some lying as they had fallen and others stacked awaiting burial. A marine bulldozer was excavating a large trench for a mass burial.

> The dead Chinese were being carried and placed into the trench as the bulldozer continued to work, increasing the size of the trench. I believe that marines were handling the dead Chinese with one marine at the head and another marine at the feet. Each dead Chinese was carried by two marines and placed, not dragged, into the trench. I do not believe that Dog Company marines were used for this burial detail.
>
> I also remember that my squad was standing by, waiting for orders to move out. The ground under my feet felt spongy, and I used the toe of my foot to push and move some of the dirt. Much to my surprise, I found that I was standing on the forehead of a dead Chinese that had been buried in a very shallow grave. Apparently, this dead Chinese had been buried during the battle.

Ron Klein, a lieutenant at the time of Operation Mousetrap and now a retired lieutenant colonel, also shared his memories:

> I very distinctly remember this because of what I saw of the aftermath. Its purpose was, I believe, explained to us in a briefing that the skipper, Al Mackin, would give us before any such planned move by our company, and that's where I first heard the term "Operation Mousetrap."
>
> As he told us, intelligence had determined that the Chinese were planning a major attack in mid-May 1951, and the Tenth Corps had decided to set up a false front and entice the CCF into attacking through it. Units of battalion and company size were to be placed on widely separated strong points and in a line

at an angle to and about a mile in front of the regular corps line, which, at the time, was the No Name Line. Our battalion was the one chosen, and we occupied a small hill and ridge complex.

The next-nearest units were a Korean Marine Corps company about a half mile off our left flank and an Army battalion the same distance away on our right. The Chinese were supposed to think they had run into our MLR (main line of resistance), find weak spots in it, and change the direction of their attack. The trap worked perfectly.

A few days after we moved into our positions, CCF attacked one night. The few troops we had in the valley to our left quickly pulled out. The CCF probed our front, found the weak spot in our left flank, and went pouring through. When they got close to the main line, they were taken under fire and found themselves in a cul-de-sac with fire from three sides. We also had a tank company in back of us in the valley that added to the devastation.

We estimated they had moved an entire regiment through the fake "gap" we had created, and there was little left of it in the morning. I saw enemy bodies stacked up along the road running through the valley, which were so numerous that tanks with bulldozer blades mounted on their fronts were pushing the bodies into a deep gully and then covering them up.

I saw a few marines walking over the bodies and was told by someone they were searching for documents or other intelligence information. I don't believe it was anyone from our company.

At a later date, while visiting an adjacent tank unit, I met a company officer that I had known at Quantico. In exchanging stories about some of our experiences, he told me he had been with the tanks that were at our left flank during Operation Mousetrap and added these two interesting stories:

The tanks were positioned in line along the edge of a road. The lead tank was in back of a small hummock with its gun pointing forward and over a long, sharp drop-off. For some reason the tanks were not protected with infantry, probably because nobody thought the enemy would get that far into the "gap" purposely left in our false "front line." But they did, and that night the tank unit found itself immersed in a flood of Chinese.

The enemy troops didn't have adequate arms to do damage to the tanks that were all buttoned up, so some tried removing the tracks from the bogie wheels. One tank was damaged when a grenade was pushed into its engine compartment. Each tank proceeded to spray its adjacent ones with its .30-caliber machine gun, swinging their turrets around as necessary. This played havoc with the Chinese, while doing no damage whatsoever to the tanks.

Most of the enemy troops that survived took off for elsewhere, but a few stuck around, some under the tanks, still trying to damage the treads without success until rooted out at daybreak.

In front of the lead tank, just below the crest of the hill, and only a few yards in front of the muzzle of the main gun, they found a Chinese soldier dug into a shallow hole. He was completely out of his head.

This poor soul had apparently worked his way toward the front of the tank just as the tank fired its .90. The blast had rolled him back down the hill, and he'd valiantly crawled up again, only to be rolled back down by the next blast. Finally, giving up, he'd dug his little hole and had lain there the rest of the night while that .90 had blasted away over his head intermittently until dawn. There's no doubt that he was not only totally deaf, but probably whacked out for the rest of his life. That .90 is *noisy.*

Did It Really Take Place?

I have always been surprised that Operation Mousetrap did not receive much publicity. Lieutenant Klein expressed similar wonder. He wrote:

> It is strange that this operation, which was highly successful, doesn't get a mention in the official reports. I can't find it in our 2nd Battalion's unit diary. I believe the action took place on the night of May 16, although it could have been the 17th.
>
> In the days prior, the diaries only refer to our movements to our positions and then later our movements back to the No Name Line. I do not have the Historical Diaries of either the 7th Marines or the 1st Division.

> I don't believe Lt. Brendan O'Donnell bothered with those because we were only interested in Dog Company. And that may explain the mystery because we were not directly engaged with the enemy."

I did find reference to it, but without the name "Mousetrap," in the "official" history—Volume IV, *The East-Central Front* of the collection *U.S. Marine Operations in Korea 1950–1953*, published by the Historical Branch, G-3, HQ USMC. The information can be found on pages 123 and 124 and on Map 12. Historians may not remember the operation, but many of us marines do.

Bud Calvin Remembers

Bud Calvin was in First Squad, First Platoon, Able Company, First Battalion, Seventh Regiment. This is what he remembers about Operation Mousetrap:

> Our company, along with Charlie Company, was pulled off the line, and we were transported about ten miles or so out in front of the front lines. Three tanks and a mortar company joined us, along with a machine-gun platoon. We dug in on the forward slope of a ridgeline that surrounded a small valley. Our company was the northern-most part of a perimeter set up around the small valley.
>
> We had been told that our planes had spotted troop movement estimated at about five thousand Chinese headed our direction. The direction they were taking would lead them between us and the front lines. When they got to that position, we were to collapse back on them, thereby the mousetrap.

The problem was that they came right into the middle of our perimeter on about the second or third night. Our mortars fired flares in addition to regular rounds, and it developed into quite a firefight. At daylight we pulled out, heading back to our lines. Someone counted that we had killed 487 Chinese that night.

We were shagging south when we learned that the First Cavalry Division (army) on our division's left flank and the ROK on the division right flank had both bugged out when the Chinese hit them. Our division had to drop back to try and establish a new front line. There were Chinese everywhere, and it took us five days and nights to get back to division.

I think it was on the second day of our getting back to our lines that our platoon was pulled out of the column, and we got on the three tanks. They hauled us over to where the First Cavalry had left their artillery pieces (all serviceable)—105s and 155s. We had to bust the breechblocks so the Chinese could not use our own weapons on us.

I remember the gunners on top of the tanks firing the .50s on the hillsides surrounding us to keep the Chinese off us until we finished our job of rendering the guns inoperative. As soon as we finished, we climbed back on the tanks and rejoined our column moving south.

There were probably more companies involved in Mousetrap, but being the most northern part of the parameter and then the rear guard when we headed south, I didn't see any other companies. That is how

> I remember Mousetrap. I know it took place in the middle of May in 1951 because after we rejoined our line, and we started moving north again, I was wounded on May 29.
>
> We got clobbered really bad on that date by mortars and machine-gun fire. I was in the aid station for five days and then rejoined my company on line. I still carry around a little mortar shrapnel today, but other than that I am in pretty good health except for my feet and legs giving a lot of trouble.
>
> I am sure others that were in Mousetrap will remember it differently, but we did our part, and that is what counts. I hope you have luck in your quest to get the straight story of Mousetrap. I know that nothing has ever been published about it in news and very, very little in books.

Another marine, William M. Park, who was a sergeant in Dog Company's First Engineer Battalion, Second Squad, Second Platoon, recalls the operation as well:

> I was part of the Second Platoon under the command of Lieutenant Javis. We traveled to a location out in front of the lines. We set up probably in the middle of this location. I talked to some marines that were setting their 60mm mortars. They explained how they set up their 60 on grid.
>
> I walked over to some tanks that were dug in, and a tanker told me that the tanks were set up on artillery grid and could hit a crossroad eighteen miles away. That night and the rest of the nights we spent at this location. A shell was fired every ten minutes all night.

I learned to go to sleep between shells and not wake or hear a shell all night.

Day 2—I went on tank patrol. We went out toward a town and turned around. We had no contact with the enemy. As we were going out, I noticed a Chinese soldier lying on his back beside the road. I noticed his eyes were still in contact.

Day 3—We went on tank patrol again. Still no contact with the enemy.

Day 4—Someone else in the platoon went on tank patrol. A Chinese officer and twenty-five of his command surrendered.

Day 5—We went on tank patrol and saw the dead Chinaman. This time the meat was starting to slip on his face. We went through a town, and on the other side of town a mine field was set. Rip and I got off the tank and disarmed the mines. One had gone off, and parts of a horse were everywhere.

We got back on the tank and went in for a mile or two and came under high velocity artillery fire. The shell landed about 100 to 150 yards away. They never corrected their fire. We turned around and went back to the minefield. We got off and were told that the last tank would pick us up. We watched it go out of sight and reset the minefield.

One mine was torn up. I placed a hand grenade under it and pulled the pin. Rip and I started walking through town. Rip was on one side, and I was on the other. When we got to the other side of town, the tankers were stopped waiting for us. We headed back to base.

On arriving, I reported to Lieutenant Javis that I had placed a grenade under one mine. We were told to load up and moved back south. It was close to dark when we got back.

I was ordered to take my machine gun and seven other engineers up a hill on the east side of the road. We dug in on a draw and set up for the night. About 0200 we heard a firefight on our left. The firefight lasted all night. At dawn, I saw the marines go down the hill. I was told this was I Company, Seventh Marines.

And the memories kept coming.

Dale Erickson Remembers

Dale Erickson, a member of the Assault Platoon, Recon Unit, and Weapons 2/7 (USMC)

in Korea 1950–51, recalls the following about Operation Mousetrap:

> In April and May we had Operation Mousetrap. During this period we were mostly on the move and on patrols. Our orders were to pull out of our forward positions after the Chinese poured down on us from the north, locate the enemy, and report their position. Marine units were strategically placed along the line in places that we had determined the Chinese would use to try to encircle us. At times we had skirmishes with their patrols.

Whoever planned this operation did an exceptional job anticipating what route the Chinese would use to attempt to encircle us. The Seventh Marines, with tanks, artillery, mortars, and air strikes, were waiting for them. When the Chinese showed up, all hell broke loose on them.

At one pass that we came upon on our way out, two marine tanks were there spaced about two hundred feet apart. The two tanks had to face each other and fire on each other when the Chinese swarmed over them. The Chinese did not let up. They just kept coming in on the two tanks, and the tankers just kept pouring it on them.

We happened to be there just after this battle took place. We saw Chinese bodies piled up around the two tanks. In one small pocket of the action that day, there must have been three hundred dead Chinese. The marines used bulldozers to bury them.

Operation Mousetrap always fascinated me. I did lots of research on this operation and never could come up with anything. The Marines that I talked to about it also talked about the large number of enemy casualties. I saw the dozers burying the Chinese bodies by the hundreds. I saw blood running down the ditches near the place where the tanks killed hundreds.

My unit took about thirty prisoners that day. We had a short firefight with them until they threw their arms away and joined in with us walking out. All of them had new uniforms, tennis shoes, and equipment with

> them like they had just arrived in Korea. Some of the Chinese that surrendered to us that day were very tall—some well over six feet.
>
> Something fascinating that day was that a small Manchurian horse joined up with us. It had gaping sores on its back. The corpsmen gave us sulfa and other meds for the horse. After a while he healed up and stayed with us for several months.

Well, Operation Mousetrap may not have made it into the history books, but a lot of marines certainly remembered it. Why not? Some of them served as bait in the trap, but they had no intention of being caught. Indeed, they didn't. The Chinese were, however, and they paid a horrible price as a result.

Dead Chinese soldiers, Operation Mouse Trap, mid-May 1951

Operation Mousetrap

Dead Chinese soldiers, mid-May 1951

Operation Mousetrap

Niles Gugliano

Fred Frankville

Fred Frankville in Pusan, December 5, 1950

Al Beahm

Captain Al Mackin, August 1951

Captured Chinese Army truck, part of Dog Company's motor pool

Left to right: Chuck Curley, Curtis L. Mason, Reginald D. Champlain, and Bill Griffin taking a ten-minute break as we fall back from the Hwachon Reservoir. The entire left flank of the UN line broke on April 22 or 23, causing the Sixth Roc division to cease to exist. The marines were ordered to fall back to a new defensive position and hold, which they did. (Photo taken April 25, 1951.)

Some of the platoon: *back row,* unknown and Bob Weidner; *middle row,* Bill Finnerty, Dick Becker, and Fred Frankville; *front row,* unknown, John Fitzgerald, Al Beahm, Evan Thomas, and Matt Davis

Matt Davis receiving his second Purple Heart, May 1951

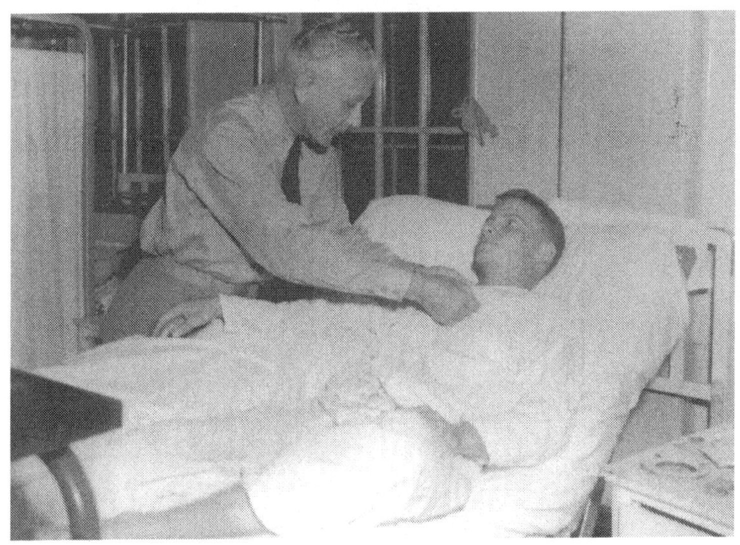

Matt Davis receiving his third Purple Heart,

Fred Frankville and Vern Firnstall

Poc Hogan and Geno Bartilato of a 4.2 mortar company

Interpreter Lim Young Soo

Korean people on my last day in Korea

Painted by Joe McKenna

Carrying Joe McKenna down Hill 753

Joe McKenna and Fred Frankville

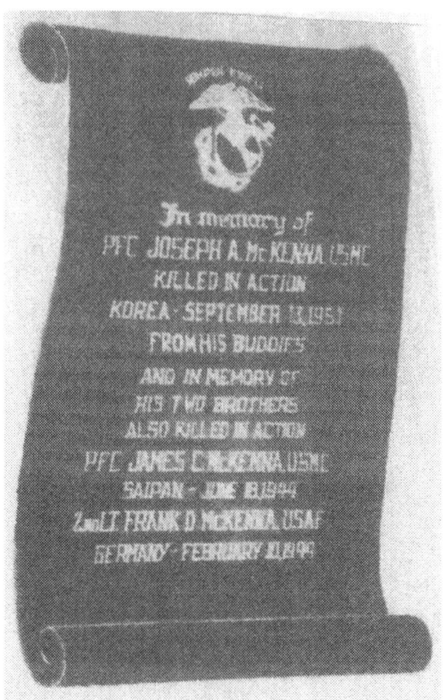

Memorial sign of the McKenna brothers who were killed in World War II and Korea. The sign is hanging at the Marine Memorial Club/Hotel in San Francisco, California.

Fred Frankville, central Korea, early spring of 1951

Fred Frankville, summer of 1951

Sergeant Robert Damon

Perry J. Dickey

Betty and Major Brendan O'Donnell

Major Brendan O'Donnell

Richard DeWert at boot camp, 1949

Garfield King, Matt Davis, Lealon Wimpee, and Fred Frankville

Graduation from boot camp forty-seven years late

Korea revisit *(left to right):* Fred Frankville, Poc Hogan, Mrs. Lim Young Soo, Al Mackin, and interpreter Lim Young Soo in 1951. Lim and his wife live in Seoul, South Korea.

Poc Hogan, November 1951

Poc Hogan and Fred Frankville

At Poc Hogan's home

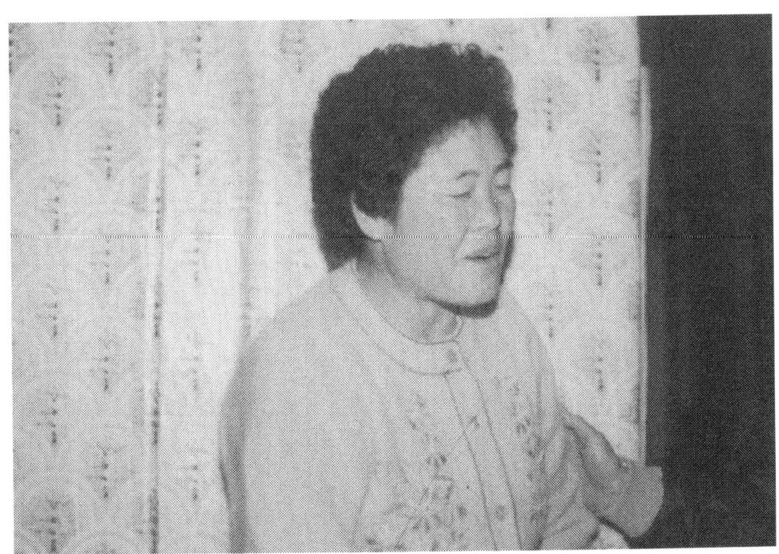

Poc Hogan's wife

Poc Hogan's mother

Poc Hogan, his mother, and his wife. Poc Hogan found his mother in 1954 three years after being lost. Poc Hogan was found alongside the road by Dog Company in September 1951.

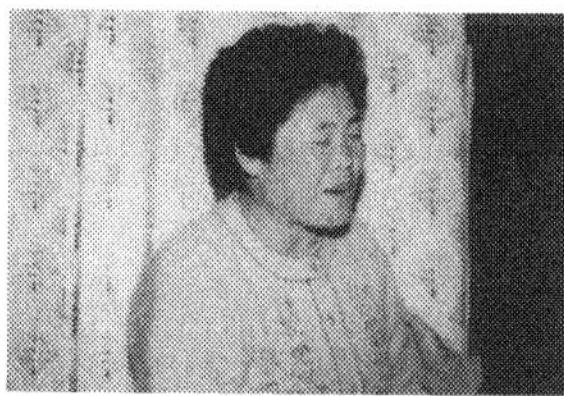

Mrs. Poc Hogan in an emotional moment

A happy Poc Hogan

Have another drink of Soju, Colonel Mackin.

Lim Young Soo and his wife and Colonel Al Mackin and his wife, Mary Mackin

A happy hostess

Left to right: Fred and Sherry Frankville, Poc Hogan, and Mary and Al Mackin. (Both these pictures were taken at the Korea revisit reception.)

At the Korea revisit reception, 1987

Fred Frankville, Mary Mackin, and Lim Young Soo at the revisit reception

Party time. A lot of personality was shown by all. We were invited to a drinking party. Fred Frankville was the last man standing. He said, "I did it for my country."

Meeting with new friends days before we left Korea

Presenting a gift to Fred Frankville (a drinking table)

Farewell salute to Fred Frankville

Korean businessman and family

Hotel attendants

Carol Wimpee and Lieutenant Colonel Lealon Wimpee at a ceremony for a Silver Star presentation on November 5, 1999, for his heroic actions taken on April 23, 1951

Lieutenant Colonel Wimpee receiving the Silver Star

United States Marine Corps

The Commanding General
Marine Corps Recruit Depot/Western Recruiting Region
takes pleasure in presenting this

Certificate of Completion

to

Fred Frankville/1119815
DOG COMPANY, 2ND BN, 7TH MARINES
for successfully completing
Marine Corps Recruit Depot, San Diego's
RECRUIT TRAINING PROGRAM
this 26th day of Sep, 19 97.

H.P. Osman
Brigadier General, U.S. Marine Corps
Commanding General, MCRD/WRR

Frederick P. Frankville's Marine Corps certificate of completion

Colonel Alvin Mackin

Left to right: Jacque Hartman, Al Mackin's daughter; Lientenant Eric Gumz, Coleen Mackin, Al Mackin's daughter; and Fred Frankville

Colonel Al Mackin's funeral at Arlington. *Front row, left to right:* Lieutenant Eric Gumz, Al's niece, and Al's daughter and son-in-law, Jacque and Robert Hartman. Back row, left to right: Janice and Charles Curley

Some of the men of Dog/7 at the dedication ceremony of the Richard DeWert Medical Clinic at Marine Cold Weather Base at Bridgeport, California *Front row, from left to right:* Colonel Al Mackin, Lieutenant Colonel Lealon Wimpee, Fred Frankville, Hans Schultz (who also served in World War II, a veteran of Iwo Jima), James Titchenal, Charles W. Curley, and Art Contreras. *Back row, from left to right:* Mel Corliss; Jack Larson; Dr. Gonzalo Garza, PhD; and Bob Squires

Chapter 13
The Spring after the Mousetrap

Laughing—but Always Close to Dying

Mousetrap ended and spring sprang. We had some amusing incidents. All they do, however, is break up the monotony of war. We could never forget that our lives hung in the balance every day.

Wimpee Was No General Sherman

Dog/7 was hiking along a dirt road behind some Korean huts with the traditional straw roofs. Up ahead we could see some smoke. Lieutenant Wimpee started running ahead of us, yelling, "Stop! Stop!" Maybe he was having flashbacks to what General William Tecumseh Sherman did to his native South almost a century earlier.

Some marines had set several roofs on fire before he could get to them and order them to stop. We took off our jackets and all of us started to beat out the flames. After a wild time, we got the fires out, but our utility jackets were a mess.

I had never seen Lieutenant Wimpee upset before. He

started yelling at the two firebugs, saying, "The Yankees did this to us during the Civil War, and I am not going to let you people do it here." Lieutenant Wimpee was a true son of the South, even if it happened to be South Korea this time.

To Walk or Ride? Dangerous Either Way

I remember Platoon Sergeant Herman Lawrence. He was too old to be traipsing around the mountains of Korea. In fact, we used to think he was as old as the mountains of Korea. I remember him telling me that in World War II he spent four years on a heavy cruiser. He didn't think that war would ever end—and he wasn't even walking far during that one.

Lawrence, who was tall and lanky, looked a bit like the actor Robert Mitchum. He could hardly get up with his pack on. If he was sitting down, we had to help him get on his feet. He had to shave almost every day. He used the last swallow of water in his canteen to shave. Lawrence had a mirror with a wood frame. In this mountain-climbing environment, every ounce of weight counted. I would have pitched that wooden-framed mirror.

On May 28, 1951, we were hiking in two columns along a dirt road, one file on each side, when several big trucks drove between us. They almost crowded us off the road. Along came a jeep with Sergeant Lawrence riding in the backseat with a pile of newspapers stacked next to him. He gave me a big smile and a little wave, proud of the fact that he had hooked a ride on the jeep. There was the driver and another passenger in the front seat.

The jeep had gone about fifty feet or so by me when there was a gigantic explosion. The others and I hit the deck, and I remember looking up and seeing newspapers floating down from above. The jeep had hit a land mine.

The trucks that preceded the jeep had wide wheel tracks that had straddled the mine. The jeep, with its narrow track, was not so lucky. We ran over to the jeep. Sergeant Lawrence was lying under it. The jeep was upside down, with the back of the jeep over him. He was in shock, and he pleaded, "Would someone please get this Jeep off of me?" We lifted it off him.

The driver was killed. The other passenger and Sergeant Lawrence were both hurt seriously. Six marines walking along the road near the jeep were wounded—several of them seriously. That was the last we saw of Sergeant Lawrence. He never came back to Dog/7. For him, that was a short and memorable ride.

Objective 8

During a mortar attack on June 10, 1951, Lieutenant Wimpee, First Lieutenant Tom Burke, and many other marines were wounded. We were short of marines because of this. Captain Mackin wrote to his wife, Mary, on June 12, 1951:

> Last Sunday (June 10th) Dog Company was ordered up a valley to attack an enemy hill from our flank. Before we jumped off I knew we were going to get clobbered. We did ... in a space of 15 minutes. I had 25 casualties, two of them serious. To boot, I lost two good officers, 1st Lt. Tom Burke, my new Exec., and 3rd platoon leader 2nd Lt. Lee Wimpee. I have lost so many men lately that I feel like an old-timer. Almost 50% of my people are bad with diarrhea or dysentery. Our combat efficiency is far below par and if we are not relieved shortly, it can prove disastrous.

Here is how it all came about:

On June 12, 1951, Easy Company was on a recon squad patrol on Objective 8 when it was ambushed. The company lost a member of the patrol in a fierce firefight and could not retrieve the body. Captain Mackin told us (the Third Platoon) that we were to go on a retrieve mission on June 13 to take Objective 8 and an adjacent hill, Able 8, and return with the body. He said that we would be getting replacements from rear support troops, clerks, postal workers, cooks, radio repairmen, etc., in the morning.

The captain said that he was going to go with us as the platoon leader. We started down the hill and hiked toward Objective 8, about an hour away. My replacement was a nice kid, about eighteen years old and as nervous as one can be with his first taste of combat pending.

I know he had heard a lot of horror stories about combat, some of them embellished to the point of fantasy. His name was Ed; he must have asked me a dozen times, "What do I do?" He also said a dozen times, "I have never been in combat. What do I do?"

I kept repeating, "I will tell you when we get there."

To Ed we must have looked like junkyard dogs. We had done this stuff so many times it was like going to work like we did back home. We had good days and bad days. The thrill for most of us was gone.

Ed, the Broken Needle

We started down our hill about 9:00 a.m., hiking about an hour or so to get to Objective 8. Ed sounded more and more like a broken needle.

My replacement marine asked me again and again, "What do I do?" Then he would say again, "I have never done this before." I told him over and over that I would tell him when we got there. On and on and on ...

When we got to the base of Objective 8, we saw that it was shaped like a hockey stick with the handle toward the base. The top had a hook. Able 8 looked like a giant cone and was right next to Objective 8. They were both wooded with low- to medium-size pine trees we could use as cover.

At first, we had not received any enemy fire that I remember. Ed asked me again what he should do. I was beginning to lose patience with him.

I said, "Ed, I want you to take a good look at me."

He said, "Okay."

Then I made him promise that he would not shoot at anyone who looked like me. Ed promised he would not shoot me. Our machine gunners started giving us overhead fire support, and I said, "Let's go."

Ed and I started walking up the hill side by side. A loud explosion on our left side knocked us over with the concussion. I asked Ed if he was hurt, and he said no.

We were both lying flat on the ground and had started to get up when we saw a smoking Russian grenade about six feet away and the North Korean soldier who apparently had tossed it moving out of sight. I put my hand on the top of Ed's helmet and shoved his head down in the dirt, along with mine.

When the grenade exploded, it sent splinters into the

back of my hand, as well as into my hip and arm. Ed said, "I am hit." I looked at his wounds, which were like mine, and, seeing that we were not hurt that bad, said, "Let's get this over. Let's go."

Ed Earns a Purple Heart

We started back up the hill side by side and saw a dead North Korean soldier in his foxhole. A little way up the hill was another dead North Korean in his foxhole, thanks to our Third Section machine gunners. None of that seemed to faze Ed.

He kept up and did what a marine does in combat. We were almost to the top of the hill when we came upon a wounded North Korean who was shot in both arms. He had a burp gun, which he tried to lift to shoot us. He could not lift the gun on account of his wounds. We watched him for a little wile with some admiration, and then I took his Russian-made gun from him. This was good trading stock. I knew the rear echelon troops would pay or trade a lot for this trophy.

We found out later that the loud explosion that knocked us down when we were starting up the hill was friendly fire. Ed and I went to the aid station to get patched up. He asked me if he would get a Purple Heart for his wounds. When I said yes, Ed was thrilled. He said that his parents were going to be so proud. I replied that he was a hero.

And he was no longer asking me, "What do I do?" He had learned quickly how to act in combat—and survive. Moreover, he had made his parents proud and earned a Purple Heart his first time in battle. It was a great day all around for Ed.

In a letter to his wife, Mary, dated June 14, 1951, Captain Mackin said, "I had to send a patrol out to Objective 8 out to our front and I decided to go along. The hill was occupied by

North Koreans. We had a fight on our hands but we charged up the hill and took it. We had five casualties—three of them from a misfire of one of our own mortars."

Ed and I were two of the five casualties. The rest were from the misfired mortar round. The company records show four casualties: Edward B. Lane, Richard O. Miller, Robert S. Sullenberger, and Fred Frankville.

It took us about forty-five minutes to take Objective 8. Ed, a company clerk who became a temporary replacement in Dog/7 for just that one day, did good work—proof that all marines are first riflemen. He would have a lot to talk about when he got home.

Ed did not return to Dog Company after treatment at the aid station. He got his wounds taken care of and went back to his clerk job as a hero and a celebrity.

Adventure at the Water Hole

We assaulted a rather high hill in the Punch Bowl area. I don't remember the elevation, but it was a long way up, and it was very hot. Before we got to the top of the hill, we were out of water.

It is hard for some people to imagine how we suffered with thirst. When we secured an objective, the first thing we did was go for water. Each squad sent a two-man team with a five-gallon can strapped to a packboard and several canteens back down the hill the same way we came up to bring back the water. This could be a five- or six-hour trip.

The marine I was to go down the hill with was Hank Blankenship. He was from the Appalachian region back in the States. He was a good, dependable marine, as were all the men from that part of the country.

The way he talked used to crack me up. He said things

like, "What went with my helmet is what went with my other stuff."

I said, "Hank, get your packboard, the water can, and some canteens. We're going after water."

He asked, "Why do we always have to get water?"

I told him it was because we didn't have any rank. He replied with logic, "People with rank drink water."

I told him that if we didn't go, we would get plenty of water—bread and water in the brig. When he said that was more than we were getting now, I had to agree.

I told him that we weren't going with the other guys for water. Instead, we were going straight down the hill to where two mountains ran together because there was usually water there. If not, we could turn toward the trail and go with the rest of the water team. If we found water, it would cut our time in half.

We started straight down, grabbing trees and shrubs and sliding, and using a little profanity along the way. In about an hour we came into a thicket that was heavy with pine trees—and water. We took off our helmets, leaned our rifles against a pine tree, took the water can and our canteens, and waded out in that cool water.

It was about ankle-deep and maybe thirty feet across. I dipped my canteen cup in this cool water and must have gulped down three canteen cups. I also poured some water on my head.

Suddenly Hank said to me, "Fred, look over there."

I looked over. Across the stream, about sixty feet or so away, were two Chinese soldiers. They had the drop on us. They must have heard us coming for some time with all that cussing we were doing while sliding down the hill.

One of the Chinese soldiers had a rifle pointed toward

us. The other was on his haunches with a bunch of canteens with straps on them, getting water. I was shocked and said to myself, "Where in the hell did they come from?"

I was staring at the guy with the rifle, wondering why he did not shoot. All the time Hank was saying over and over, "We are dead."

The Chinese soldier who had the rifle stopped aiming it at us. I said, "Hank, fill your can and canteens up. Then we will go over and get our gear and leave."

He said, "They'll shoot us."

I told him that if they were going to do that, we would have been dead when we showed up.

"We will get our water," I declared.

We put on our gear and walked away. The pine tree cover was so thick that we disappeared quickly. I think we flew up the hill.

We got a break. Apparently, there was peace at the water hole, if not in the rest of Korea.

What If the Canteen Had Been on the Other Belt?

When we got to the top of the hill, the guys lined up for a drink. We had beaten the other water carriers back by several hours.

After our squad got their canteens full, we started to loan out water by the swallow. We gave other marines three swallows and tried to be fair because they were dying for water.

When the other water carriers got back, they paid us back. I told our platoon about our adventure at the water hole. The Chinese were there first but didn't shoot us.

Our platoon leader said, "They'll get another chance in the morning when we take our next objective."

I will never forget those Chinese soldiers. I wondered what I would have done if the tables were turned.

A Bitter Taste in Captain Mackin's Mouth

Captain Mackin wrote to his wife, Mary, on June 20, 1951: "In the last 12 days we have had 66 casualties—two killed and one lost both legs. The replacements and the Marines who were wounded and returning are in better health than the Marines who stayed with the company."

He also wrote that he was bitter about the conditions his men were living in and the lack of relief. It rained so hard that we were actually flooded out of our foxholes.

I can relate to the conditions that Captain Mackin was writing about. We were dug in on the forward slope, and the rain ran in and filled up our foxholes. We had to use our helmets as bailing buckets.

The flies were unbearable. If we opened up a can of C rations, the flies covered our spoon of food before we could eat any of it. There were millions of little green frogs with red bellies (we called them Chinese frogs), and they jumped all over the place—even on the hillsides. They jumped on us when we tried to sleep.

Mother Nature was against us. If we had been in the army, we would have been sent to Japan for two weeks after six months on line. In Japan, we would be getting back to civilization. We would have clean bodies and clean clothes, and we would be sitting at a table with a tablecloth, eating lobster and steak or a hamburger, and sipping a nice drink.

For marine infantry, it was not to be.

Chapter 14
The War Drags On

A Warm Place for a Cold Marine

Other marine units had rest and recreation (R & R) and lived a more humanlike lifestyle than we did. Once, in March 1951, we went to a rest area near where marine forward air controllers were stationed. We saw a tent out in the field with a stovepipe sticking out of the top. Anything with a heating stove in it created curiosity to us "Ice Marines."

We walked over. The structure was a toilet with a stove in it so the users wouldn't get their butts cold. Once we discovered that, we moved in en masse. The air controllers could not use the facilities without stepping on us.

Their colonel made a deal with our CO that if we would move out of their toilet, he would give us a squad tent minus the stove. We agreed and managed to liberate some of their food rations like bread, milk, bacon, and peanut butter. The airmen also got R & R—what a difference in the lifestyle of marine units.

An Expensive Frisbee Game

We stayed on this ridge for a week or so, waiting for the flanks to catch up. We seemed to always be waiting for the flanks to catch up after we took an objective. The mail clerk came up and said we had a crate at the bottom of the hill that was very heavy, and he needed three or four guys to lug it up the hill. The crate was from John Fielding, a member of our squad.

Fielding had gotten very sick several weeks before and was evacuated to Japan for treatment. Before he was evacuated, we had all gathered around him and put in our order for stuff that we wanted him to send us from Japan—stuff like whiskey, brandy, cans of lobster, shrimp, chocolate, boneless chicken, and other delicacies. We could only hope ...

Four of us took a packboard and went down the hill to pick up our crate of goodies. It was very heavy, but thinking about the contents gave us extra energy.

It took about two hours of huffing and puffing to reach the top of the hill. We set the crate down, took out our bayonets, and pried the boards off the box. We cleaned some straw off the top of our crate and looked inside. Our emotions went downhill immediately ... from jubilation to devastation.

Instead of the whiskey, chocolate, etc., that we had anticipated, the crate was filled with Noritake china. The irony was not lost on us. We spent our days fighting Chinese, and here was another serving of china that we neither needed nor wanted.

The shipping clerk in Japan had sent our crate to John's mother, and we got hers. We took the Noritake plates, ate some C rations and canned beans off of them, and then used them for Frisbees. It was a world record—the first Frisbee game played with Noritake china in the summer of 1951 at twenty-seven hundred feet on a mountaintop in Korea during wartime.

Several days later a copter flew up the mountainside with a cargo net with supplies such as water, food, ammunition, and mail. The days of being marine mules were mostly over. The Marine Corps was using helicopters to replace human laborers. What a relief.

Target Practice

We heard some rifle fire to our left. Lieutenant Wimpee asked me to go with him to investigate. A rifle platoon from our company was firing down the hillside like target practice. We found a rifleman shooting down the hillside at a wounded Chinese soldier, and an officer with field glasses who was checking the rifleman's marksmanship—telling him things like, "Too far to the left" or "too low."

Lieutenant Wimpee got very upset. He told the officer (a first lieutenant) to stop what he was doing. They got in a heated argument. They were nose-to-nose and almost came to blows.

Lieutenant Wimpee was made of the right stuff. His mother was a World War I French war bride and his father was an American soldier who was a member of an Alabama artillery unit using 75mm guns. This three-inch, fast-firing gun was close to the front lines and was considered to be most in harm's way due to its limited range.

The lieutenant's father and mother met in a nearby village. After he married her, she moved to the United States. They lived in Alabama and had five children. Lee Wimpee's desire was always to take his mother back to France to meet her family. However, this was not meant to be. She died in the late 1950s.

Captain Mackin walked over, stopped the argument, and told Lieutenant Wimpee to take a corpsman and go down the hill to check out the Chinese soldier. The Chinese and North Koreans often left their seriously wounded out in front of our lines for medical treatment. This enemy soldier had a piece of his skull missing. It looked like a small triangle, and we could see his brain.

The corpsman put a bandage on his head, gave him a shot of something, and radioed for someone to pick him up.

The Chinese and North Koreans had limited medical facilities to care for the seriously wounded. Oftentimes they would bring their badly wounded during the night hours and leave them in front of our lines hoping that we would treat them. I saw them leave badly burned soldiers—burnt by napalm from air attacks. They were actually burned black, with their skin blistered off.

I remember one Chinese soldier with half of his jaw missing. From the center of his chin to his left ear was missing. His tongue was hanging out alongside of what was left of his face. Some marine gave him a piece of orange candy, and the wounded and disfigured enemy soldier attempted to eat it.

Last Punch Bowl Objective

On June 20, 1951, Dog/7 secured its last objective in our part of the Punch Bowl campaign. It was the end of seventy-three days of eating C ration canned beans, canned hash, and bad-tasting beef stew. It's a wonder we didn't have scurvy eating this junk. We got every other disease imaginable living in the filth of Korea.

We were in a reserve area near a river with a sandy beach. We all went swimming to wash the crud out of our clothes and soak layers of dirt off ourselves. We felt like we had been recycled. We had a field kitchen that served real food, and all we cared to eat. We felt like we were on vacation.

The first few days in reserve, we were left alone to sleep, rest, write letters, and check out our new surroundings. We found out that our neighbor in this rest area was the Ninth Regiment of the Second Army Division. This was like finding the "mother lode." The army had so much stuff, and we were so poor that it was hard to believe we were part of the same country. We just helped ourselves to the necessities, such as clothing, food, machine guns, packboards, and an occasional jeep.

Captain Mackin wrote to his wife, Mary:

> We are in this new area located next to the Army 9th Regiment of the 2nd Army Division. As a general rule, the Army is always loaded down with all sorts of gear that a Marine would give his eye-teeth for.
>
> Marines are noted for their "acquisition facilities," commonly known as scrounging. Naturally when they spotted a lot of gear lying around in the neighbor's yard they lost no time in requisitioning it. ... They almost stole the Army blind.
>
> Three times a day I have had Army representatives come to me and report equipment that has been stolen. "Borrowed" sounds better. They are very nice about the whole thing. Fortunately, we recovered all the missing gear. It embarrassed the hell out of me because they treated us royally insofar as giving chow to my people and outfitting them with clothing articles.
>
> We also "acquired" packboards that were 100 percent

better than the backpacks we marines used. The backpacks had straps that cut into our shoulders. The packboards we "acquired" were distributed among the marines before the army knew that they were missing. We were the first marine unit that had packboards, courtesy of the US Army, and we kept them.

Ironically, in World War I, the Fifth and Sixth Marine Regiments were part of the Second Army Division. The marine regiments made history at Belleau Wood while being part of the Second Division. This history lives on as one of the marines' greatest military achievements. Major General John A. Lejeune, after whom the Marine Corps base in North Carolina is named, and where the Second Marine Division is located, was commanding General of the Army's Second Division from mid-1918 to mid-1919. It was the first time that a marine commanded an army division.

Bootleg Whiskey

A Korean civilian work party was at our swimming hole. They were working on some construction project when two of the Korean laborers approached us with two bottles of whiskey for sale. One of the bottles was labeled "Three Roses" and the other "Four Feathers." What was wrong with that picture?

Back in the USA, the label was just the opposite: "Four Roses" and "Three Feathers." One of the guys bought a bottle of this stuff. He said it tasted horrible, but he kept on drinking it. He offered the rest of us a drink, but we turned him down.

After a few drinks, he started to get sick. Then he started to throw up a lot. He got deathly sick. The corpsman said he was poisoned and gave him some stuff to drink. The next day he was not much better. I thought he was going to go to some hospital facility for treatment, but he started to feel a little better that night. The next day he was sitting up saying, "If I ever see that bootlegging SOB again, I am going to shoot him."

He no sooner said that when in came the friendly bootlegger, all smiles and carrying a bottle of Three Roses. He also had a friend with him.

I said, "Here comes your favorite bartender."

The marine jumped up, grabbed his M-1 rifle, and jammed it into the Korean's stomach. He took the bottle of Three Roses, twisted the cap off, and made the Korean drink it.

The Korean protested, but the marine poked the rifle into his midsection and forced him to drink. The Korean was drinking and gagging and choking. He fell down on his rear and continued to drink under the threat of death. He then started to vomit and roll on the ground. The other Korean took him under the arms and dragged him out of sight.

That ended the bootlegging business, at least around our part of the camp.

Jack Benny Arrives—and We Put on a Show

On July 3, 1951, Jack Benny and his troupe, including Errol Flynn and Marjorie Reynolds, put on a show. We were all looking forward to it. Hundreds of troops showed up, including ones from the army, Marine Corps, and air force. Flynn got to ride a helicopter and flew all over the show. A lot of pretty women sang and made jokes with Jack Benny. It was a great performance that was very entertaining. It sure beat fighting the Chinese and North Koreans.

A few days later we gave a live-fire demonstration for some army and Marine Corps brass: General James Van Fleet, General "Ned" Almond, and General Carthrae Thomas, the commander of the First Marine Division. Also, some civilian dignitaries were present. As usual, when the brass wanted a show, we became the actors.

We started training the next day with reveille at 5:00 a.m. We attacked a make-believe enemy in a make-believe position and then repeated the process and went to chow. At dusk we started training for night operations. The following days we repeated this process all over.

We all thought that we were being trained to make night attacks, which would be something new for us, because the commies attacked at night, and we attacked in the daylight. We made another live-fire demonstration after dark for some army and marine brass. It was just like a Hollywood war movie for the visitors.

For us, it was kind of fun, especially since we knew there were no live enemies shooting back at us.

Beefing Up Their Defenses

We left our bivouac area near the Hwachon Reservoir on July 16 and moved south about forty-three miles to a point on the outskirts of Hongchon. We were now behind the lines, or "in the rear with the gear" in military parlance

The peace talks were going on. In the past, when the commies wanted to talk peace, that meant the war was not going well for them. When that happened, they asked for a reprieve from the war and said they wanted to talk peace. Our politicians always agreed and halted our attacks.

The Communists then used this time to beef up their defense. I didn't think that we should agree to peace talks while we were winning. But the political and military leaders didn't often—if ever—solicit the opinions of the troops on either side who actually did the fighting and the dying. So they just continued talking futilely among themselves.

When the talks failed, as they always did, we attacked against defenses that were murder—and we paid the price. Those were the times when there were real enemies ahead, behind, and all around us—and leaders like Generals Van Fleet, and Almond were generally nowhere to be found.

Chapter 15
South Korean Marine Corps and Drinks Galore

Surprise, Surprise: The Sergeant Speaks Japanese

The South Korean Marine Corps was second to none. They were so much more professional than the South Korean army that the comparison was negligible. They were part of our First Marine Division, and they were 100 percent reliable. I heard that the officers were Japanese World War II veterans.

From time to time we sent a US Marine liaison over to them to instruct them as to our tactics. During our time in reserve, Lieutenant Wimpee and Sergeant Gonzalo Garza went to pay the Korean marines a visit and to instruct them on the latest US Marine doctrine.

After they introduced themselves to the Koreans, some of the Korean officers talking Japanese to each other said some derogatory and insulting things about the Americans. Sergeant Garza went to Japanese language school during World War II and understood what they were saying. He answered the Koreans back in Japanese and returned the same derogatory insults back to them. Needless to say, they were in shock and apologetic.

Lieutenant Wimpee also was surprised to know that Sergeant Garza could speak Japanese and was proud of the fact that he put the Japanese-speaking officers in their place.

The Korean marine major was a Manchurian who only spoke Japanese and Chinese. He was talking to his troops in Japanese when off to the side he noticed a young lieutenant standing in the rain with a bright yellow raincoat. The major went over to the young officer, tore his raincoat off of him, and tore it to pieces. The young lieutenant stood ramrod straight during this abuse.

Discipline in the Korean Marine Corps was severe. I personally witnessed an officer beating an enlisted man with a rifle butt, and the Korean marine stood the abuse without a whimper.

Sergeant Garza stated that the Korean Marine Corps unit that he and Lieutenant Wimpee visited was commanded by a Manchurian. This is true in part. When I was talking to retired Sergeant Major John Hernstrom, whom I have known since the Korean War, he told me that officers and radiomen in the Korean marines were all Japanese. In fact, he revealed, he had been assigned to the Korean Marine Corps as a forward observer for artillery for over three months.

When the Japanese invaded and conquered Manchuria in 1932, they changed the name to Manchukuo. They made Manchukuo a satellite country and gave it sovereignty under that name. This new country had several mercenary units. One of them was White Russian from World War I. The

Koreans, as well, had a mercenary unit. The Japanese unit was named "Kando," a notorious group.

When the Russians conquered Manchukuo in August 1945, they returned this area to the Chinese. The White Russians went to Australia, and the Japanese were deported to Japan or South Korea. There were as many as five hundred thousand. The first two commanders of the Korean marines came from the Kando special unit. They also brought with them their radiomen of the same Japanese ethnic makeup. They called themselves Manchurians for political reasons. We had not yet signed the peace treaty with Japan.

When discussing the ROK Marines' role in the Korean War, fellow marine Reinhold "Ron" Klein recounted this story:

> Just to confirm and add to your comments on the KMC, Wimpee also told me the story about the major, the second lieutenant, and the yellow raincoat. He told me that many of their NCOs were also Japanese, and that there was bad blood between the Japanese and the Koreans because of the former having occupied Korea during or before World War II.
>
> We always admired and sometimes were in awe of the Korean Marine Corps. During the Chinese Spring Offense in April of 1951 they were on the right flank of the First Marine Division, between us and the US Second Army Division, and they held the line while the Second had to withdraw. That, of course, happened on our left flank also when two ROK regiments bugged out, leaving Able Company, First Battalion, Seventh Marines to hold the line alone.
>
> Somewhere in my Korean recollections I mention the occasion when Dog Company was on the line

adjacent to a KMC unit. We were sitting on a ridge just a couple hundred yards from another ridge in front of us. A KMC platoon had been ordered to advance and attempt to take and occupy a portion of the forward ridge while we were watching them. What we saw was almost unbelievable.

They got about halfway to the top when they started getting small-arms and automatic weapons fire. At this point they were on a small bare knoll and were obviously slowing down. Suddenly their platoon leader strode into the middle of the knoll and started shouting at them, which caused them to sit down in a wide circle around him.

He began walking around the inside of the circle yelling at and berating his men. We couldn't make out the words, but he was obviously unhappy with their lack of progress. All this time we could see the dirt spouting up from the bullets that were hitting all around them. How he managed to ignore them I don't know, but when he apparently felt he had the attention of his men, he shouted a loud order that must have meant "Charge," because his whole platoon jumped to their feet and, with a screeching yell, ran up the hill the rest of the way and took the ridge. And we thought we were gung ho!

Lucky in Life, Unlucky with Beer

After about three weeks in reserve, we were getting bored with all the training. We old-timers didn't need it; however, the replacements fresh out of boot camp benefited from it.

We used to get replacements while we were on line. I

always thought that it was too much of a shock to jump into combat without any familiarization and bonding with the new men. Captain Mackin knew that too. He always greeted the new replacements by saying, "Welcome to the family of Dog/7. I know you will all do well, and we are proud to have you as the new members of our family." That had a positive impact on all of us, especially on our critical bonding process.

One day in the chow line we each got two large scoops of ice cream. This was the first ice cream that I had had in a year. We also got two cans of warm Lucky Lager beer. The print on the can told consumers that they were lucky if they lived in Seattle, Washington, where this beer was made. Maybe they were lucky because they had a way to keep their beer cold.

It was about ninety degrees in Korea, and we had no ice to cool the beer. I punched a hole in my hot can to taste the beer. Foam squirted out, and the can was almost emptied of its contents. The beer tasted bitter and hot. I sold my other can to a guy for a dollar.

Kool-Aid Becomes a Cool Aid

We also got a can of orange juice from the Women's Christian Temperance Union. We could almost always get as many apples and oranges as we wanted.

I remember getting a half a loaf of unsliced bread, as well as butter and jelly. We did not get any soda pop.

At the time, Lieutenant Wimpee did not drink beer, and he told me that he sure would like an ice-cold bottle of Coke. He said it had been months since he had one. I admitted to him that it was longer for me and that I had two packs of strawberry Kool-Aid on me, but I didn't have any sugar for it. He volunteered to look for some.

Lieutenant Wimpee later showed up with a carton full of sugar. We went to a stream of water, took the liners out of our helmets, put two Halazone tablets in the helmets, filled up one helmet with water, poured the water/Kool-Aid mix from one helmet to the other, and had a Kool-Aid party. Kool-Aid never tasted better.

Peep Show

We pulled up roots from this location and went north again to our first reserve area after we left the front lines. It seemed that the Tenth Corps commander wanted us close to the front lines in the event that he needed us. The cease-fire was still in effect, but there was no trusting the commies. People were still getting killed by land mines—ours and the enemy's. We still had to go on recon patrols to police the "no-man's-land" between the lines.

The Third Platoon that I was in went out on a recon patrol one very hot day. We started out from the west end of the valley. A village was there, but we found it unoccupied. We continued walking toward the east end of the valley, toward another village about a five-mile hike from the village on the west. We went through the houses, which also seemed to be empty. "Seemed to be" often led to deadly traps for us.

Suddenly, I saw a woman run behind one of the huts. Two of us ran behind the hut and found two women there. They had seen us and had dropped to their knees in prayer fashion. They started crying and rocking back and forth with their hands clasped in a prayer mode.

One of the women was old and small; the other one was young—about nineteen or twenty years old. We tried to calm them down, but our efforts seemed to make their fears worse. The old lady said something to the young woman, and then the young woman got up, took off her dress, laid it down on the ground, and lay on the dress spread-eagle style. By then, more marines showed up, and they stared at the two crying women—the one on the ground naked, and the old one rocking back and forth.

Lieutenant Wimpee and our interpreter, Lim Young Soo, walked over to the now rather large group of marines. He looked at the woman lying on the ground naked and the old woman who was kneeling, crying and praying. With a shocked look on his face, he said, "What in the world is going on here?"

I said that I didn't know. "That woman on the ground took one look at me and took her clothes off," I explained.

The marine standing next to me said it was his handlebar mustache that made her undress. The interpreter talked to them, and they told him that they had family in the hills. They had come back to the village to get a bag of dried peas because they were starving. The Chinese told them that the Americans would rape them and kill them if they were captured. They said they wanted to live and would do whatever to stay alive. That is why the young one undressed.

When they found out that we were not going to rape or kill them, and when we all donated most of our C rations to them, they kissed our hands and did a lot of bowing. This time the tears in their eyes were tears of joy. Then we started joking to them, knowing they could not understand English.

We said things like, "I would like to meet your folks," "I will pick you up tonight in my Bentley," or "I will meet you tonight down by the rice paddy. Bring a friend, but don't bring that old one." We had fun with this patrol for days after. I don't know if they did, but at least they were alive and well-fed to discuss it with their friends and relatives.

Most of all, they were able to impart the message that we weren't as bad as the Chinese said we were. Score a public-relations victory for our side!

Captain Mackin Is about to Lose Control

Captain Mackin sent this note home to his wife about this time:

> The Division has instituted a new policy whereby any officer who serves four months in a line company is to be rotated to a (rear) job. Any man, they figure, who lasts longer is tempting fate. With respect to me, it means I have about 3 weeks to go.
>
> I'll hate to lose command of this company. They're a wonderful bunch of kids. One becomes very attached to a unit like this. I've lived with them; I've seen them fight; I've seen them hurt and die—they're like my family. In fact, when I get new replacements I give them a little (welcome aboard) speech and ask them to become part of our family.
>
> Do you understand me? It's hard to explain in words alone.

He didn't know that we felt the same way, although marines don't admit that to one another until long after they have gone their separate ways, which we and Captain Mackin did shortly thereafter.

Chapter 16
War without Captain Mackin

Lieutenant Flynn Joins the Marines

During the first week of September 1951, Captain Mackin transferred to Heavy Weapons Company, Second Battalion, where he was placed in charge of heavy mortars, heavy machine guns, and flamethrowers. He was also the weapons coordinator of supporting artillery. Lieutenant Wimpee transferred to 81mm mortars.

Our new platoon commander, Second Lieutenant Clare E. Flynn, a former navy ensign who transferred to the Marine Corps, wanted to be the best he could be and wanted his marines to know that he cared about them and was willing to learn from them.

I Join Easy/7 but Stay with D/7

Marine infantrymen expected to be transferred to a rear unit out of harm's way after nine months in a line company—if they were lucky enough to survive. I had managed to do that, so I transferred to S-2 (intelligence) and was assigned to

Easy Company, Seventh Marines, a sister infantry company. Technically, as I explained to my brother, I was in two companies at the same time.

On September 26, 1951, in a letter I wrote to my brother Don, who was stationed at Camp Roberts, California, I told him that I was transferred to H&S Company, Second Battalion, Seventh Marines, as an S2 agent on September 13. As I said, the new address didn't mean that I moved away. I was still in Dog/7 as well as E/7 as an S/2 intelligence agent. The bad part was that most of the time I had to make every other recon patrol.

I shared this patrol duty with the other S2 agent. Most of the time there were two of us per company. The patrols in this mountainous terrain were exhausting. In the summer months they were longer because of the longer daylight hours.

As part of our duties, we counted both our and the enemy's casualties. We tagged prisoners of war with red tags, asked them a few basic questions, and many times sent them down the mountain unescorted, hoping that no one shot them on their journey. We made reports to the senior S2 agent down the hill at H&S headquarters as to the results of the patrols and casualties and other things of interest. I never saw or met the senior S2 agent who was my boss. We did all of our communicating by field telephone.

Welcome to Easy/7

Two of us went down the hill and reported to a major who had on new dungarees. He looked us over and said that we looked like a couple of tramps. I told him that we were the best dressed up there. He had a point.

We were dressed in rags. We had no seats in our pants, the knees of our dungarees were worn out, and our clothes were filthy. He told us to take showers and get some new utilities, new shoes, and helmet covers. This was the first time since I had been in Korea that I had a new clothing outfit, one that was not preowned.

It was a good feeling to look and feel clean. We checked in the next morning to get our new assignment. I think the major disliked me, even though he didn't know a thing about me. So all I got out of nine months in the infantry in Dog Company was a shower and some new clothing.

I started up the hill to my new assignment at Easy/7. To say that I was unhappy would be putting it mildly. After about a four-hour walk I went to see the company CO and check in. He was sitting on a fold-up canvas chair that looked like a director's chair. His name was Schmidt.

The CO asked me what state I was from. I admitted that I was from Illinois. He said that he was too. He had been raised in Chicago and had gone to the University of Notre Dame. He was a big guy and seemed friendly enough. I found out later that he was a little hard on the junior officers.

Anyway, it was back to the war for me.

Kanmubong Ridge

Our objective was called Kanmubong Ridge. This huge ridge was located about forty miles north of the 38th parallel and included Hills 749 and 812. (The numbers meant meters high. A meter is approximately 1.1 yards.) The Seventh Marines' objective was Hill 749; the First Marines' objective was Hill 812.

Just prior to our advance, there had been a thirty-day cease-fire, during which the commies had thirty days to fortify the ridge. We in the ranks knew two things: that the enemy had asked for a cease-fire so they could fortify possible objectives and that our politicians were idiots for granting it.

This was an important battle, and we knew it was going to be costly. The Communists wanted to keep us from taking this ridgeline because it was an invasion route to North Korea. The North Koreans were well-equipped and fought fiercely.

On September 13 we started toward our objective, walking up the ridgeline toward Hill 749. All three companies of the Second Battalion had a piece of this hill. The ridges were devoid of vegetation because of the napalm and artillery that had plastered the ridges earlier.

After a while, we took a break on the ridge we were on. It was very hot, and the company ahead of us stopped because of the resistance they encountered. We were all on the side of the ridge, sitting on the trail and leaning on our packs. I was looking at the ridge about four hundred to five hundred yards away, wishing I was home having a cool drink.

As I stared at the opposite ridge, I could see people walking downhill on the ridge. I yelled out, "Gooks!" We all saw them jump into their foxholes.

I thought someone would say, "Get on the other side of the ridge." No one did. I saw enemy machine gunners setting up their guns on the forward slope. To me it was madness. We were sitting ducks.

Target Practice, and We're the Targets

The opposing ridgeline lit up with yellow-green flashes, the colors of Russian tracers, which the enemies were using. The North Koreans' bullets were hitting targets. The forward observer's radioman next to me was hit. I was outlined with bullets. The forward observer and I grabbed the radioman's arms and dragged him on the other side out of harm's way.

We got our wounded, moved to the reverse side, and called in artillery and mortar fire on the North Koreans. While other marines cleaned out the North Koreans, we continued toward our objective and got involved in some heavy combat.

My personal story is limited in particular to my experiences as S-2 in the Second Battalion's E/7 and later in D/7, and to the Seventh Marines in general. Without reading the excellent article "Kanmubong Ridge: Final Marine Offensive of the Korean War," by Colonel Joseph H. Alexander (USMC, ret.), I would not have known the detailed history of the First and Fifth Marine Regiments in this battle. (See Appendix C.)

I can personally relate to the very steep hills that we encountered. I know about "Luke the Gook's Castle" because it was the last hill I looked up at when I left Korea on November 27, 1951. It went straight up and looked down on the Seventh Marines. And it was in North Korean hands.

The division intelligence officer said that we were facing two North Korean divisions, both freshly rebuilt and supplied. They fought like Japanese. The First NKP Division would defend the high ground, and elements of the Forty-Fifth NKP Division would help defend Hill 749. I don't know how the intelligence people got this information, but they were usually right. The Reds told their troops everything. If a few were captured, we could usually find out what they were up to.

A Classic Case of a Rock and a Hard Place

Hill 749 dominated the eastern end of Kanmubong Ridge. It was surrounded by a river on three sides; the hills had steep slopes and vine-covered ravines that proved ideal for defense.

The North Koreans knew we were coming and had been

preparing defensive positions for months. Some of their bunkers were carved out of solid rock. They would be a good target for napalm, but our air support was hijacked by the air force, which wanted to use the planes for interdiction, not close troop support.

The very steep inclines made climbing extremely difficult and, in some cases, near impossible, without mountain climbing gear. It was like Luke the Gook's Castle. The castle went up from a 45 percent incline to almost straight up. We couldn't capture what we couldn't climb. The steep hills proved to be man-eaters.

The 2/7 Marines under the command of Lieutenant Colonel Louis C. Griffins were preparing for a night attack against the NKP defenders of Hill 673. On the night of September 11–12, Lieutenant Colonel Griffin led his 2/7 Marines up a stream bed that separated Hill 749 from Hill 812. The marines slogged up the stream in the dark and went undetected.

At daybreak, 2/7 came out of the early dawn and routed the NKP defenders. Across the valley, 3/7 overcame NKP defenders on Hill 680. This was done at a high cost—22 killed and 245 wounded marines in two days.

By nightfall of September 13, the First Marines arrived, and we were relieved. The Seventh Marines pulled back to division reserve at Wontang. The Seventh Marines put up a flanking defense in case the NKP and Chinese attacked our flanks.

On the night of the thirteenth, after we were relieved, Easy/7 hiked in the dark to our new defensive positions, and we got lost. We were in "no-man's-land" in the dark between two opposing forces. If the NKP or Chinese found out about our location, they would rain mortar fire on us. If the marines thought we were the enemy, we would be history.

When we got close to the marine defenses, Captain Schmidt, by himself, walked up to the marine lines. Immediately, several illuminating grenades lit up the night. We could see Captain Schmidt silhouetted against the light. Just one trigger-happy marine was all it would have taken to kill him.

To me, this was a very brave thing to do. Captain Schmidt took responsibility for being lost and took the chance that he did because he thought he was responsible and should take the risk. Most company commanders would have asked for volunteers or instructed a fire team to make contact.

PFC Matt Davis: A Magnet for Enemy Ammo

One of my closest friends, Matt Davis, a Chosin Reservoir veteran, was one of the marines wounded in the battle at Kanmubong. He had been wounded twice before. The third time was no charm for him, as Private First Class Robert Weidner, who rescued Davis at Kanmubong, suggested.

> As a member of the Third Platoon, Dog Company Seventh Marines, my squad was assigned to a recon patrol toward enemy forces on September 6, 1951. There were nine rifle squads in a company. Patrols were made on a rotation basis. We were to seek out North Korean forces dug in on Konmubong Ridge area. Dog Company had a squad recon patrol every day on line, and it was our turn to seek out the enemy.

I was the fire team leader of the point-fire team of the patrol. We assumed it was going to be another routine stroll up one of the many hills in Korea.

Captain Mackin was uncomfortable about the safety of the patrol. He told me it was the fourth time that he was instructed to send a patrol on the same route as before. He said it was conceivable the patrol would be ambushed. We were engaging North Koreans, and they were more aggressive than the Chinese Army.

The patrol was out of sight quickly on account of the rather heavy vegetation in the area. Shortly after the patrol was out of sight, we could hear heavy machine-gun fire. The patrol was ambushed.

We were climbing up this particular hill single file when suddenly what sounded like a .50-caliber machine gun opened on our squad. Instinct kicked in, and we all hit the deck with bullets striking all around us. PFC Matt Davis, who had been walking in front of me, ended up on the turf above me on the slope of the hill.

Mike Kamenca was lying above Davis. Matt's foot was positioned on top of my helmet. All of a sudden, Matt let out a yell. He flipped over on his stomach and started to roll down the side of the hill.

I yelled at Kamenca, "Matt has been hit, and I'm going down after him." I asked him for help, since he was nearest to me and also Matt's good friend.

The machine gun was firing at us as we slid down the hill toward Matt. Once down the hill, we found Matt. Luckily, we were out of sight of the enemy gunners. I took Matt's battle dressing out of his belt and attempted to stop the bleeding where the bullets had entered. Kamenca and I carried Matt to the rear, and the rest of the patrol followed. We later learned that Matt was evacuated.

Mackin's Worst Fears Are Realized

I was next to Captain Mackin waiting for the patrol to return when he said this was what he was afraid of. The North Koreans had set up an ambush before the patrol got to them.

We saw three marines headed our way. They were Weidner and Komenca carrying Matt Davis. We ran out to help them. We carried Matt Davis and Evan Thomas, who was also wounded, to a helicopter that was waiting for the wounded. I looked at Matt's face as we put him on the helicopter, and his gums were white—a sign he had done a lot of bleeding.

When the helicopter left for the medical station, the corpsman who helped with the wounded told me Matt would be dead before the helicopter got to the hospital. By some miracle, Matt lived. He was a true warrior.

Davis had been wounded at the Chosen Reservoir. No sooner had he been released from the hospital than he demanded to get back to Dog Company. Shortly thereafter, he was wounded for the second time and then released from the hospital. Following that, he was assigned to a rear echelon noncombat unit with all the safety and creature comforts. Again, he demanded to return to Dog/7 and live in the dirt with all the risks that went with combat infantry.

Davis turned down a chance to return home on the point system. This almost cost Matt his life. Thanks to Weidner and Kamenca, he lived to a relatively ripe old age. (He died in 1987.) Weidner and Kamenca risked their lives by charging through enemy machine-gun fire to rescue Matt Davis and carry him to safety. They probably would have done the same thing for any wounded marine. That is what *esprit de corps* is all about, as members of D/2/7 proved over and over again in Korea—and other marines have been doing since November 10, 1775, when the Marine Corps was established.

A Walking Miracle

Private First Class Robert Miller, also a member of the same patrol during which Davis was wounded, became a walking miracle. He came back from the patrol carrying his cartridge belt and no helmet. The machine-gun crew that hit Matt Davis and Evan Thomas hit Miller's cartridge belt and tore it off his waist.

A bullet also hit his chin strap where it was fastened to his helmet. It ripped the helmet off his head. The helmet then rolled down the hillside. It had done what helmets were designed to do: save the wearer's life—in this case, the life of the company's party.

Robert Miller was the platoon clown. He liked to imitate Charlie Chaplin and walk with his feet pointed outward and his hat on sideways. That day he lost all of his humor. He was in shock that he was still alive.

Chapter 17
War Is Unkind to Both Sides

PFCs Aren't Sergeants

Most of our squad leaders were privates first class. They should have been sergeants. Our fire-team leaders were PFCs. They should have been corporals. Our platoon right guides were corporals. They should have been sergeants. Our platoon sergeants had three stripes. They should have had four stripes.

Captain Mackin and the other officers were upset about this, and they brought it to the colonel's attention. It did not seem to do much good. The rule was one must have an accepted time in grade before he moves up to the next rank. This would have been okay if it wasn't for the casualties in the line companies that moved people of lesser rank to a higher leadership position with the added responsibilities without the rank or the pay.

What Captain Mackin did to keep experienced leadership in higher slots was to use the seniority method. If a replacement came with higher rank and he had no combat experience, he would follow a leader with lesser rank.

At one time I had two corporals and a sergeant as part of my squad. I was a squad leader even though I was a PFC. Similar situations existed in machine-gun squads.

The Sheep Don't Need a Shepherd

Around the end of October 1951, Captain Mackin, who was CO of 4.2 mortars at the time, received a letter from Lieutenant General Shepherd, US Marine Corps. This letter upset the captain.

Shepherd was visiting Tripler Army Hospital in Honolulu, where he chatted with Matt Davis. The general wanted to know why Davis, who had been wounded three times, was still a PFC.

Shepherd wrote:

24 October 1951

Dear Captain Mackin,

I am writing you concerning Private First Class Matt M. Davis 111, 1107845/0311, USMC who passed through Tripler Army Hospital here in Honolulu late last week. Available records indicate that Private First Class Davis departed from the continental United States in October 1950, served with "D" Company, 2nd Battalion, 7th Marines, and was wounded in action on 27 November 1950, 10 June 1951, and for the third time 6 September 1951, to his recent evacuation to the United States.

In the course of my conversation with this boy he told me that he had been considered for promotion to the rank of Corporal on several occasions, but that the arrival of corporal replacements within the company precluded his actual promotion. Davis impressed me as being a fine young Marine and I would like to recommend him for promotion to corporal. He mentioned that you were his commanding officer during a part of the time he served with "D" Company.

I realize that first impressions are not always correct but in view of Davis' combat service and the fact that he has been wounded three times, I would welcome your comments concerning this and whether or not he was considered for promotion to Corporal.

Very truly yours

Lemuel C. Shepherd, Jr.

Lieutenant General, U.S. Marine Corps

A letter like that from a general to a captain, however courteous it sounded, implied more than a simple question about whether Davis had been considered. It was tantamount to an order to find a way to promote him. That is what upset Captain Mackin more than anything else: there were many other marines in his command who merited promotions, some before Davis. He still had a war to fight, and administrative matters had to take a backseat. Worse, some of his marines were still dying, which upset him as well. One of them was a young man named Joe McKenna.

Back to the "Dogs"

On September 14, 1951, while I was dug in with E/7 on a hill near Kanmubong Ridge, Captain Alvin Mackin, the commander of Heavy Weapons Company, walked through our position looking for places to set up his heavy machine guns and 81mm mortars. He saw me and asked what I was doing in Easy Company.

I told him that I got transferred to the rear and ended up in E/7 as the S-2 agent. He said, "What a dirty deal after what you have been through. If you are going to be up here, you're coming with me."

Mackin talked to Captain Schmidt and said he would trade the Dog Company S-2 for me. Dog Company was short the Third Platoon leader because Second Lieutenant Flynn had been wounded on Hill 749. First Lieutenant Tom Burke, the current company commander of Dog/7, was short of officers, and Al Mackin was a welcome help. They consummated the deal, and I was back home with Dog Company.

I went to look up my good buddy, Joe McKenna. No one knew what happened to him. We checked aid stations, MASH units, Easy Med, and the hospital ships. No record of Joe. He had to be up on Hill 749, where the company had been engaged in some heavy fighting.

Leave No Marine Behind

One of the hallmarks of the Marine Corps is its dedication to a singular principle: leave no marine behind. Marines will go to extraordinary lengths to make sure, as far as is humanly possible, to bring every one of their comrades out of a battle, dead or alive.

For example, when the marines were fighting their way

to safety in the November-December battle at the Chosin Reservoir in North Korea, they did so while escorting truckloads of their frozen, dead comrades. They were not going to leave them behind in the frozen mountains of North Korea—or anyplace else—if they could avoid it.

We got an eight-man search party to look for Joe. Al Mackin gave me permission to go. Lieutenant McKay went with us.

The Fifth Marines were on the trail going to Hill 749. As we walked by them, they must have asked us a hundred times who we were and what we were doing up there. We told them over and over. When we got near to the top of Hill 749, we started to search for Joe where he had been seen last.

Dick Curtin, who was with Joe when they were attacking the hill, said it was about where we were standing that they got hit with multiple grenades. He was right. We found Joe almost immediately. He was lying face down in the bushes. He had been killed instantly.

There was a grenade shrapnel hole in back of his head just underneath his helmet. Joe had lain there for four days. In the heavy combat, he was missed and overlooked. We put Joe on the stretcher and took turns carrying him down the hill. It was sad, even for us battle-hardened marines.

The Joe McKenna Story

Private First Class Joseph Andre McKenna was born May 5, 1931. He was a graduate of Mission High School in San Francisco, California. Joe was a track star in high school, joining the United States Marine Corps after graduating with the class of 1949.

Two of his brothers were killed in World War II. His brother Frank was a second lieutenant in the Army Air Corps when he was killed over Germany in 1944. Four months later, his brother James was killed on the beach at Saipan while serving with the marines. A third brother, Leo, was wounded on Guadalcanal. Joe also lost an uncle who was serving with the marines in the South Pacific.

Since he had lost more than one brother in combat, Joe was exempt from military service. He did not have to be in harm's way in Korea. "I don't know why he did it," said his twin sister, Mary McKenna McFadden. "Life was very quiet after that."

Their father was in the Veterans Hospital in Livermore, California, with tuberculosis when Joe was killed. What was left of the McKenna family drove to the hospital to break the news of Joe's death to him.

Describing her father's agonized response, Mary said he told his wife, Artemise Latulipe McKenna, "Well, Mother, I guess we didn't teach our kids to duck." Mary McKenna McFadden had ten children to make up for the three bothers and an uncle killed in combat.

Me and Joe

In the morning hours of September 13, 1951, I had met Joe on the trail near our objective, Hill 749. This was my first day as S-2 assigned to Easy/7. Joe and I talked a little about the premonition he was having that he was going to be killed in this operation.

He said that his parents would not be able to handle his death. That is when he told me about his two brothers who were killed in World War II. I told him that being killed in combat was for other people, not for guys like us.

Joe was visibly shaken. Several hours later, Joe was killed. I think of Joe often. He was a special kid—always happy—and his mother and girlfriend sent him more packages than anyone in the platoon. After he was killed, his mother continued to send cookies to the platoon.

Joe was engaged to a girl in San Francisco. His girlfriend had a girlfriend who started to write to me. After a couple of weeks of letter writing, Joe was killed. I wrote his girlfriend a letter about Joe's death. Then I stopped writing to the girl who was writing to me. She wrote me several letters, but we stopped corresponding. I just did not know what to say. I still don't.

End of Offensive Operations

One of the reasons the Seventh Marines were replaced by the First Marines in the Kanmubong Ridge Battle was because the Seventh Marines had more time on line than any regiment—some seventy-three days. That is why the trade was made.

The Seventh Marines were involved in some of the heaviest fighting at the ridge. Two of our members received the Medal of Honor posthumously: Second Lieutenant George H. Ramer of Item Company 3/7 and Sergeant Frederick W. Mausert III of Baker Company 1/7. Both received their awards for their roles in the desperate point-blank fighting on Hills 680 and 673.

Fox Company, receiving the brunt of an attack and not giving an inch, was sparked by the incredible performance of Browning Automatic Rifleman Joseph Vittori, Fox Company 2/1, who fought a single-handed battle, bounding from flank to flank and mounting personal counter attacks. His courage kept the point position intact and prevented the entire battalion from collapsing. Vittori earned the Medal of Honor for his exploits. His citation is almost unbelievable.

*Vittori, Joseph

Rank and organization: Corporal, U.S. Marine Corps Reserve, Company F, 2d Battalion, 1st Marines, 1st Marine Division (Rein.). Place and date: Hill 749, Korea, 15 and 16 September 1951. Entered service at: Beverly, Mass. Born: 1 August 1929, Beverly, Mass.

Citation:

For conspicuous gallantry and intrepidity at the risk of his life above and beyond the call of duty while serving as an automatic-rifleman in Company F, in action against enemy aggressor forces. With a forward platoon suffering heavy casualties and forced to withdraw under a vicious enemy counterattack as his company assaulted strong hostile forces entrenched on Hill 749, Cpl. Vittori boldly rushed through the withdrawing troops with 2 other volunteers from his reserve platoon and plunged directly into the midst of the enemy. Overwhelming them in a fierce hand-to-hand struggle, he enabled his company to consolidate its positions to meet further imminent onslaughts. Quick to respond to an urgent call for a rifleman to defend a heavy machinegun positioned on the extreme point of the northern flank and virtually isolated from the remainder of the unit when the enemy again struck in force during the night, he assumed position under the devastating barrage and, fighting a single-handed battle, leaped from 1 flank to the other, covering each foxhole in turn as casualties continued to mount manning a machinegun when the gunner was struck down and making repeated trips through the heaviest shellfire to replenish ammunition. With the situation becoming extremely critical, reinforcing units to the rear pinned down under the blistering attack and foxholes left practically void by dead and wounded for a distance of 100 yards, Cpl. Vittori continued his valiant stand, refusing to give ground as the enemy penetrated to within feet of his position, simulating strength in the line and denying the foe physical occupation of the ground. Mortally wounded by the enemy machinegun and rifle bullets while persisting in his magnificent defense of the sector where approximately 200 enemy dead were found the following morning, Cpl. Vittori, by his fortitude, stouthearted courage, and great personal valor, had kept the point position intact despite the tremendous odds and undoubtedly prevented the entire battalion position from collapsing. His extraordinary heroism throughout the furious nightlong battle reflects the highest credit upon himself and the U.S. Naval Service. He gallantly gave his life for his country.

Private First Class Edward Gomez of Easy 2/1 also earned the Medal of Honor for his exploits at Kanmubong Ridge. On September 14, 1951, he threw himself on a grenade to save his machine-gun crew and preserve the position during a North Korean counterattack.

*Gomez, Edward

Rank and organization: Private First Class, U.S. Marine Corps, Reserve, Company E, 2d Battalion, 1st Marines, 1st Marine Division (Rein.). Place and date: Korea, Hill 749, 14 September 1951. Entered service at: Omaha, Neb. Born: 10 August 1932, Omaha, Neb.

Citation:

For conspicuous gallantry and intrepidity at the risk of his life above and beyond the call of duty while serving as an ammunition bearer in Company E, in action against enemy aggressor forces. Boldly advancing with his squad in support of a group of riflemen assaulting a series of strongly fortified and bitterly defended hostile positions on Hill 749, Pfc. Gomez consistently exposed himself to the withering barrage to keep his machinegun supplied with ammunition during the drive forward to seize the objective. As his squad deployed to meet an imminent counterattack, he voluntarily moved down an abandoned trench to search for a new location for the gun and, when a hostile grenade landed between him and his weapon, shouted a warning to those around him as he grasped the activated charge in his hand. Determined to save his comrades, he unhesitatingly chose to sacrifice himself and, diving into the ditch with the deadly missile, absorbed the shattering violence of the explosion in his body. By his stouthearted courage, incomparable valor, and decisive spirit of self-sacrifice, Pfc. Gomez inspired the others to heroic efforts in subsequently repelling the outnumbering foe, and his valiant conduct throughout sustained and enhanced the finest traditions of the U.S. Naval Service. He gallantly gave his life for his country.

The First Marines suffered most of the casualties in the last four days at Kanmubong Ridge, where 850 of them were killed or wounded. Lieutenant Colonel Houston Stiff of 2/5 took the lead against Hill 812. When supporting air force air attacks proved, in his words, to be exasperatingly unreliable, he clobbered the hill with every available ground weapon—artillery, tanks, recoilless rifles, rocket trucks, and heavy mortars.

Eventually, the Fifth Marines overwhelmed the stunned survivors of the First NKP Division on Hill 812. But, to the west, an ugly granite rock called "Luke the Gook's Castle" was not taken because it was simply too steep to climb. General Thomas called off all advances against the NKP forces per directive from General Van Fleet. Van Fleet said it was unprofitable to continue the bitter operation.

This end of the fighting at Kanmubong Ridge marked the termination of offensive marine operations for the rest of the war. For the next twenty-two months they would engage in trench and outpost war.

A Steep Price for a Steep Hill

The long fight for Hill 749 had enabled the Allies to add a forty-five-hundred-yard bulge in the lines, for whatever that was worth. The North Korean forces likely lost twenty-five hundred killed. (Remember, the Communists never released casualty specifics.) The First Marine Division's 1,950 casualties included 254 dead.

Some twenty-two thousand Americans became casualties in this type of fighting from August to October 1951. The losses were sustained in an effort to merely straighten the lines, not to win anything—and we didn't want to upset the Russians.

This shocked the folks back home. In a poll taken in October 1951, the public said that this was a senseless and useless war. General Thomas was bitter about the loss of so many of his men. He blamed unsatisfactory air support and not receiving permission for an amphibious operation for the outcome of the battle.

The Marines left Kanmubong Ridge with a bad taste. Marine Corps historian Ralph Donnelly wrote that Kanmubong Ridge was one of the hardest offensive operations ever mounted by the First Marine Division. If we had our air wing under our command, and if they had let General Thomas make an amphibious landing behind the ridge, this would have been a successful operation with limited casualties.

Unfortunately, people in other branches of the military, as well as politicians who were in power, would not let the marines fight as marines. They dismantled the greatest fighting force in the world, and they had no shame.

The "Ridge" Changed the North Koreans Too

Kanmubong Ridge also changed the way the North Koreans fought the war. They changed their tactics there. When we had attacked them earlier in the war, they holed up in their foxholes and bunkers and fought a defensive battle—in most cases to the death. At this battle, they started coming out of their defensive positions and counterattacked.

I remember firing into groups of them. They would meet our attacks head-on. This was not all bad, because it exposed them to our firepower. However, it showed a more aggressive form of combat.

As I have already mentioned, I was in S-2 (intelligence) assigned to E/7. My job was, in part, to count the enemy dead and captured and our dead and wounded. It was not a pleasant job counting our dead. Some of the dead marines looked like high school kids. Those who were killed instantly had a wide-eyed look of shock on their faces. I remember one dead marine who stared at me as I was checking his dog tag.

After all these years I can still see him—and the faces of too many young people, friends and enemies alike. War is unkind to both sides.

Chapter 18
My Part of the War Ends

A Little Boy Left Behind

In the late summer and early fall period of 1951, Dog/7 moved up to engage enemy forces that had broken through ROK units. We walked through refugees going in the opposite direction fleeing the Chinese. The shared road was packed with women, children, and men.

After struggling to get by them and walking for a couple of miles, we found a little boy alongside the road, screaming his head off. He was left by the refugees in their haste to get away from the fighting.

Poc Hogan

We were infantry loaded down with guns and ammo and had no means of transportation, except walking. Nevertheless, we could not leave him there, or he would die. Captain Mackin said, "Let's take him with us."

We took turns carrying the boy. We gave him some of our C ration candy and food, and he started smiling and calmed down. He fell asleep in our arms. He quickly became one of us.

In effect, we took this little guy to war. We kept him in the rear of the column, put a helmet on him, and dug him in with the company headquarters. Since we were near a town named Poc Hogan that is what we named him. Later, we got him clothes that fit. Poc was a fun kid—always happy. He was destined to become even happier.

Poc found his family four years after the war. When my wife Sherry and I went to Korea compliments of the Korean government in 1987, there to greet us was Poc Hogan, all grown up and very emotional. We met his wife and mother. I took a lot of pictures.

Mackin, Poc, and I Join 4.2 Mortars

On October 10, 1951, Captain Mackin packed up his gear. He told me he was going to be transferred as the CO of a 4.2 mortar company. He informed me that he was going to sleep on a cot in a tent with a stove, where there was a real mess hall with a cook on duty all the time. And, he stressed, he was going to have bacon and eggs and toast in the morning.

I said to him, "You lucky guy."

He replied, "So are you. You are going with me. Get Poc Hogan, and let's go."

In the previous two months Captain Mackin had gone from CO of Dog/7 to CO of Weapons Company to CO of S2 (intelligence) and now to CO of a 4.2 mortar company. That meant that he was going to be promoted to major. I was happy to go with him no matter what his rank was.

We hiked down the hill toward the 4.2 mortar compound, which was about an hour away. From the hillside it looked like a hobo camp. The mortar men took the empty ammo boxes apart and made wooden shanties with the boards. There were also some squad tents and a large tent with the sides' open, which was the mess tent.

"Atten-shun"

While Captain Mackin introduced himself to the other officers, I took Poc Hogan and went to the mess tent. I asked the cook if he had anything like sweet rolls or pancakes. He said he had some pancake batter. In a couple of minutes Poc Hogan and I were eating pancakes with a lot of syrup. Poc Hogan thought he was in heaven, and so did I.

Captain Mackin came back and joined us and told me that I was going to be his jeep driver. He said that my tent was right behind us and told me to fit Poc Hogan in wherever he would fit.

After we ate, I took Poc Hogan, and we walked into the tent. There were twelve guys there, all lying on their backs on their cots. All twelve of them jumped up on their feet and then did a 180-degree turn with their backs to us. We were being shunned.

I was upset and lost my temper. I said some harsh words to the whole group. One marine said to me that he was a sergeant and that I couldn't talk to him that way. I said, "When the captain finds out how you have treated us, I am going to outrank you."

Captain Mackin entered the tent in the middle of this heated conversation. In an instant there was complete silence. Captain Mackin asked my permission to use the jeep because he and the exec wanted to drive around the area. I had yet to see the jeep, but I agreed that he could take it.

The twelve guys in the tent were all in shock about the request. They told me that the position of jeep driver was a status position given on a seniority basis and that I had crashed the party. I said, "The captain wants to be his own driver. Why don't you shun him?"

Guard for Hire

After that blowup we all got to be friends. We fitted another cot in the tent for Poc Hogan; he was living in luxury.

I seldom drove the jeep because Captain Mackin liked to drive it himself. As a result, my time with 4.2 was easy living. I even found a part-time job.

I hired myself out for outpost duty. Everyone had to take turns on outpost duty. In that area, it was a relatively safe job. No one got by the infantry that was protecting us, but every unit had outpost watch. For five dollars I would take their place. It was easy money.

Five bucks was two days' pay. The word was out that nobody had to spend two Christmases in Korea, so that meant that I was a short-timer. Just like when I was a kid, I couldn't wait for Christmas.

A Whiskey-Producing Orange Tree

A marine in the unit was way over six feet tall. His name was Geno Bortalotto. He got a big can of orange juice in the mail and asked me if I would like a taste of this special orange juice.

"What's so special about it?" I asked.

He peeled the label off the can and showed me a spot of solder on the side of the can. He said his dad owned a liquor store in New Jersey. His dad would empty the juice out, fill the can with whiskey, solder the hole, put the label back, and send the can to his son in Korea.

What a great gift that was!

One More Encounter with Luke's Castle

The road out of the 4.2 mortar compound to the ocean went by the fortress we had named Luke the Gook's Castle. It was a huge, steep, ugly rock fortress that went straight up. We never captured it because of its features, even though the North Koreans used it to call in artillery fire on us. It was virtually impregnable.

The battleship USS *New Jersey* delivered supporting fire on Luke's Castle. The three-thousand-pound shells would hit the castle, and the ground would quiver, but the castle would still be there. But I wasn't much longer.

On November 27, 1951, we were told that some trucks would pick up the marines going home and take them to the beach to board a ship. We were to be ready. About 10:00 a.m. the trucks stopped by the 4.2 mortars and picked some of us up, including Captain Mackin. I could not believe I was leaving this place alive.

I can't relate how happy I was to get to this point. Our convoy of trucks with troops from various companies of the Second Battalion was on the move toward the ocean. When we got opposite Luke's Castle, the truck I was riding on stopped running. That was a bad omen.

I just knew the North Koreans would call artillery or mortar fire on us, and I would not make it home. The truck in front of us stopped, backed up, tied a chain to our truck, and towed us away. It was unbelievable that we received no hostile fire.

My Last Day in Korea Includes a Lot of Welcome Baloney

My last day in Korea was miserable. I was cold and hungry, which was nothing new. But I was going home to get warm.

When we got to the beach, they took our cold-weather gear—parkas, field-jacket liners, and more—from us, even though the temperature was two degrees below zero, and the wind was blowing fiercely off the ocean.

The LST (landing ship tank)that was to pick us up and take us to a ship anchored quite a way out in the ocean ran aground about a half mile from the beach. Because the LST was grounded, they started using two LCVP(landing craft vehicle personnel) boats for transport to the ship. Each one was supposed to hold about thirty troops, but we squeezed in about fifty per boat.

About two thousand marines and soldiers were on the beach awaiting transport. With no cold-weather clothing to protect us, and a long way to the ship, we were freezing. Captain Mackin talked to the truck drivers, all of whom gave us some gasoline and buckets. We filled the buckets with sand, poured gasoline in the buckets of sand, and started fires. It was what kept us from freezing.

When we finally got on board the ship, the sailors told us that we could turn right when we got below and get cleaned up—or go to the left toward the food that was set up for us. We were covered with soot from the gasoline fires, and we looked like a minstrel show, but we all headed for the food.

There were piles of baloney sandwiches on white bread and coffee. When I picked up my first sandwich, it was covered with my black fingerprints before I could eat it, but this did not slow me down a bit. On my next sandwich, the fingerprints were not so pronounced.

Marines Should Not Wear Lipstick

The ship we were on headed for Kobe, Japan. We learned that we were going to the port of Kobe, then to Otsu to get physicals and our sea bags, and then board another ship in a few days and head for home. The plan was to get us home before Christmas 1951. Since it was November 28, there was not much time.

When we got to Kobe, we boarded a train for Otsu and an old Japanese army base where we left our sea bags with our uniforms. We all took physicals; I did all right. Some others had a little problem with worms. After we got in uniform, we got permission to leave the base. It was too late to go to Kobe, so we thought we might explore Otsu.

Otsu was a small town with not much going on. Another marine and I were milling around the front gate thinking about going to town when a pedal cab pulled up. This was a little carriage pulled by a bicycle. The driver asked if we wanted a ride to town, and he kept repeating the word "lipstick" over and over.

We thought he was going to take us to a geisha house. I had never been to one, but I heard that they were elegant and that the women wore kimonos and had big hairdos. The marine with me was a big guy, and the carriage went down the road sideways. We went into a dark and smoky part of town where dogs were barking.

The driver stopped in front of a gated wall. The gate opened, and an old lady started talking to the driver. She motioned to us to follow her, which we did. We went into the house, took off our shoes, and sat on two pillows on the floor.

The old lady bowed to us and said, "Lipstick," several times. The door across the room opened up, and two skinny little girls showed up covered with lipstick. They didn't have a boob on them, and they looked like little boys.

The marine next to me asked, "Which one do you want?"

I said, "This is your lucky day. You can have them both."

He left the room with one of them. I was alone in the room with the other girl and the old woman. I refused to go with the girl.

I shook my head, saying, "No, no."

The old woman pointed toward the lips and said over and over, "Lipstick, lipstick."

I said no. The girl started crying, and the old lady started wringing her hands. I took some money out and paid them for services not rendered, but the girl continued to cry.

On the way back to the base, the big Marine asked me why I did not take the girl. I said I paid as much for not doing it as he had for doing it—and I would have paid more.

I told him, "It's been a long time for me, and when I get a woman, she is going to look like one."

Meeting the "Pope"

The day after I swore off lipstick, we went to Kobe. We visited a big hotel run by the US Navy. It was a nice place where we could get the best dinner for ten cents. I had steak, shrimp, and champagne. That was a great way to prepare for a long ocean voyage.

The next day we boarded the USNS *General Pope.* It was a beautiful, twelve-thousand-ton, large, roomy ship. That did not matter to me at the time. I would have been happy to board a leaky bathtub if it was heading back to the United States.

The *Pope* was a World War II–era vessel. Then it was fitted out to carry five thousand troops. After the war it had been converted to a more comfortable ship that was used to move military families with children around the world. It had a big play area for kids with a swing set, sliding boards, and a sandbox.

The ship was not crowded, so we could sleep anyplace we wanted. The food was great, and I did not get seasick. It looked like I would be home for Christmas. What a great feeling! The hardest part for me in Korea had been being homesick. The cure was on the horizon, which we kept sailing toward.

San Francisco—and Home

My record of service shows that I arrived at the marine base at San Francisco on December 20, 1951. My previous record shows that I left Korea on November 27. What happened to the twenty-three days in between and the troop ship *General Pope* was not mentioned. I wonder how I got to San Francisco. Kobe, Japan, or when I left Japan was not mentioned either.

The next day was even more confusing. When the paymaster paid me, I was shorted six months' pay. I had not been paid for over a year, and I should have had this back pay on the books.

In retrospect, what I thought had been a great deal in skipping boot camp may not have been such a smart move after all since I was not paid for my first six months of service. I put in a claim for my pay later, but after arriving in "Frisco," all I wanted was enough money to buy a train ticket. I had gotten out of Korea with what I wanted most—my butt. That was back pay enough for the time being.

I boarded a train out of San Francisco for Galesburg, Illinois, in the early afternoon on the twenty-first of December. If all went as planned, I figured that I would be home on the twenty-third of December. For one of the few times in my life, I was right.

Chapter 19
Home at Last

Getting Off in Galesburg

Galesburg was about forty miles from my hometown of Rock Island, Illinois. My mother, dad, and brother John were going to pick me up. About an hour out of Galesburg, I started to walk back and forth from one coach to the other. I was so keyed up I could not sit down. When I got off the train, my mother let out a scream and hugged and kissed me. It was the most emotional time in my life.

This was my first day home in eighteen months. In all that time I had only had two days liberty, in Japan, while being processed to come home. I really needed some time to unwind. I think I had a drink with all my old friends and some new ones. I liked waking up in my old bed, getting up when I wanted to, and not having to carry a weapon every place I went—at least temporarily.

Easy Company Wasn't All That Easy

I still had my enlistment to complete. On January 24, 1952, I was assigned to Easy Company, Eighth Marines, Second Division, and stationed at Camp Lejeune, North Carolina. I was in another infantry company, which was horrible.

After a regular day of trooping and stomping, we fell out after evening chow and went on night problems through the swamps. Then we went back to the barracks by 10:00 p.m., got cleaned up, and started over at five thirty the next morning.

The whole company wanted to volunteer to go to Korea, but when they asked my opinion, I told them, "Here they can abuse you, but they won't kill you."

I did not like the stateside Marine Corps. People were rank happy. In Korea, the job a marine had was based on seniority. Rank was secondary, and a marine had to have a specific time in grade to get promoted. The high number casualties meant the corps had to use marines of lower rank for higher positions.

I was a squad leader, and I was only a private first class. PFCs were also machine-gun section leaders. It was a crazy setup. By contrast, in the army, if a soldier had a job, he was also given the rank that went with it. That was not the only difference between stateside and Korea, though—which got me into a bit of hot water at times.

Not going to boot camp made me lax on military courtesy. I got chewed out a few times for not saluting officers. Korea was a saluting-free zone. Therefore, not thinking about where I was, I extended my nonsaluting practice to Camp Lejeune. Nevertheless, I survived Camp Lejeune—and it survived me.

Check, Mate

I was released from active duty on February 12, 1952, and went back in the reserves. When I got home, I wrote a letter to the commandant about the six months' pay that I was shorted. I told him that I got a Silver Star and a Purple Heart and that I had earned it.

About two weeks later I got an envelope addressed from the commandant of the Marine Corps. In the envelope was a check but no letter. A letter would have been nice, but a check was what I wanted.

Do They Have to Eliminate the Marine Corps Because I Left?

President Harry S. Truman, who presided over the Korean War, was never a fan of the United States Marine Corps. As he said, "The Marine Corps is the navy's police force, and as long as I am president, that is what it will remain. They have a propaganda machine that is almost equal to Stalin's." He would live to eat those words.

The nation's second secretary of defense, Louis A. Johnson, entered office sharing President Truman's commitment to achieve further military unification, reduce budget expenditures on defense, and get rid of the Marine Corps. Truman was known to approach defense budgetary requests in abstract without regard to defense response requirements in the event of conflicts with potential enemies. From the beginning Johnson and Truman assumed that the United States' monopoly on the atomic bomb was adequate protection against any and all external threats.

Johnson promptly began proposing mothballing or scrapping much of the surface fleet and amphibious forces.

Johnson had a conversation with Admiral Richard A. Connally in which he gave a revealing look at his attitudes toward the navy and Marine Corps.

"The navy is on its way out. There is no reason for having a navy and a Marine Corps ... Army General Bradley tells me amphibious operations are a thing of the past. We will never have any more amphibious operations. That does away the Marine Corps, and the air force can do anything the navy can do so that does away with the navy."

Johnson attempted to eliminate the Marine Corps' aviation branch, transferring its assets to other services. He also proposed eliminating the marines altogether in a series of budget cutbacks and ordered the commandant of the Marine Corps be deleted from the official role of chiefs of services branches.

At that time all heads of services were authorized to have a driver. As a cost-cutting measure—as well as an insult to the Marine Corps—Johnson cut the marines out of this motor pool. Johnson also attempted to eliminate the celebration of the Marine Corps birthday.

A short time after he called the Marine Corps a police force and likened its PR machine to Stalin's, the marines he disliked so much showed the world how American marines can fight. They showed the world at the Pusan Perimeter at Inchon, at the Chosen Reservoir. When the Eighth Army made the longest retreat in US military history, the marines called the rush south by the US Army "the Great Bug Out."

One marine division destroyed a Chinese army and kept the commies off the Eighth Army's back as they retreated south. One marine division showed the world what American boys properly led can do under extreme conditions. This operation and the drive north from Pohang in southeast

Korea to Wonju and on to Hoengsong in Central Korea—then to the east coast to Kanmubong Ridge, and then across the Korean peninsula to the west coast to defend Seoul—saved the Marine Corps forever.

Congress stepped in and passed an act declaring that there will be three marine divisions and supporting arms forever. Johnson resigned on September 19, 1950. President Truman apologized for insulting the Marine Corps. The marines told Harry to take a hike.

The United States Marine Corps helped save Korea, and the Korean War saved the United States Marine Corps. The First Marine Division was the SWAT team of the Korean War. It was a brutal, primitive, infantry war, fought in an environment in which the marines could—and did—fight well. I was proud to be part of it.

Casualties in First Marine Division History

The Marine Corps paid a price in human blood for its participation in the Korean War, as it did in every war before and since. According to an article in the August 2007 *VFW Magazine*, the First Marine Division "sustained the most combat deaths of any U.S. Army or Marine division during WWII in the Pacific Theater with 3,470 KIA and 14,438 WIA." During the three-year Korean War, the total division casualties were 4,004 KIA and 25,864 WIA.

From 1965 to 1969, the First Marine Division sustained more than six thousand KIA in Vietnam. Eight marines were killed in the defense of Saudi Arabia and the Persian Gulf in 1990–91. In Somalia (December 1992 to April 27, 1993), two marines were KIA, and nine were WIA.

The marine casualty total thus far (this memoir was written in 2010) in Iraq and Afghanistan has not yet been determined because casualties are still happening. By far the marines who served in Korea suffered the greater number of casualties in the shortest length of time.

Boot Camp Graduate—Forty-Seven Years Later

I attended a Dog 7, Marine Corps, reunion in San Diego, California, on September 26, 1997. We watched marine recruits graduating from boot camp in a beautiful ceremony. To our surprise, about twenty-five former members of Dog Company, Seventh Marines, who were in attendance, were called forward. We received certificates of graduation along with the new recruits, who were now called marines. The certificate was signed by H. P. Osman, brigadier general, US Marine Corps commanding general, MCRD/WAR.

I was honored to be among these fine young men. It took me forty-seven years and two months to graduate from boot-camp training. You might say I was a slow learner! And I even got to fight in a war without it.

Chapter 20
Back to Korea

Back to Where I Never Wanted to Go

When I left Korea, I never envisioned going back. But when the opportunity arose, I returned. And I kept track of some of my old buddies from my Korean War days, especially Captain Al Mackin. He had been among the troops' favorite officers in Korea. He remained so until his death in 2010.

The Captain and I Return

Al Mackin stayed in the active Marine Reserve after the Korean War and rose to the rank of full colonel. I called him every New Year's Day for more than fifty years. My wife, Sherry, and I also visited with Colonel Mackin and his wife, Mary. On one of our visits he said that he kept a correspondence going with our old interpreter, Lim Young Soo, who lives in Seoul. Lim said we should pay Korea a visit.

The Korean government sponsored a revisit program through which it paid a hefty part of veterans' expenses if they returned. We agreed that we should take advantage of the offer to visit Korea for a one-week, all-expenses-paid trip. There was no limit to the South Korean government's appreciation for what troops from twenty-one nations had done to save its country.

We all agreed to visit Korea in the late summer of 1987. Al Mackin passed the word to Lim that we would meet him at the hotel we were booked to stay in and the time of our arrival. We also told him that it would be great if he could locate Poc Hogan, the little kid we picked up alongside the road in late September 1951.

A Shocking Reaction

When we landed in Korea and walked through the airport, I was in shock. The airport was out of fantasyland. It was super modern and was staffed by well-dressed and polite people. We drove through Seoul past modern buildings lining a six-lane highway, which was about five more lanes than we had seen in the country a mere thirty-six years earlier. We saw Colonel Sanders, Dunkin' Donuts, McDonald's, and other franchise stores along the route. The country was not just "rebuilt"—it was brand-new. South Korea had gone from the Stone Age to the twenty-first century in less than half a century!

We met Lim Young Soo and his wife at the hotel. They had located Poc Hogan and brought him along. He was all grown up—which was not surprising, since we had not seen him for thirty-six years. Needless to say, it was a very emotional time for all of us.

When we checked in at the hotel, we all received a book of food tickets. The value of the tickets was more than we could eat. It was good at the many hotel restaurants, which included the Parisian Room, the Venetian Room, and the

Chicago Room—and they were on just one level. The large international continuous buffet, which included lobster and champagne, was located in the lower level.

Poc Hogan wanted us to go to his house and meet his family, including his mother, whom he found three years after the war ended. The Korean government made great efforts to reunite families, and Poc Hogan was lucky—he found his family. We made plans to visit Poc Hogan's farm.

The "Seoul" of Korea

The next morning we all boarded a tour bus to see the sights of Seoul. The city was very impressive. It looked brand-new and spotless. The Korean people were very gracious and grateful. It was an interesting time, and statues of General MacArthur were at several places. The Koreans loved this general. We kept our opinions to ourselves.

The next day we skipped the tour bus and hired a van with a driver to go to Poc Hogan's place, about ten miles from our hotel. This had to be the most emotional time for Poc Hogan and his family ever.

When we arrived at Poc Hogan's farm, which comprised about eight acres, we were met by his wife, who was about as nervous as a hostess could be. We also met his mother, who was very quiet and reserved.

Poc Hogan was elated that this was taking place. It was a storybook meeting. Who could imagine that something like this was taking place? Only thirty-six years before, Dog Company Seventh Marines picked up this screaming little boy alongside a dusty road. He had been separated from his fleeing refugee family, and he was alone.

The refugees were running away from the Chinese commies, and Dog/7 Marines were heading toward the commies to stop them. Poc Hogan heard the sounds of combat that night and the next day. We protected the lad by placing him in the rear of the company, as much out of harm's way as we could.

He was a happy kid, grateful for any special treatment that he was shown—like receiving all the candy that we got with our C rations. Less than a month later, Captain Mackin was made CO of a 4.2 mortar company and took Poc Hogan and me with him. We went from living in the dirt to a "five-star resort"—a tent with a stove, a cot, and all the food and good stuff we wanted.

The mortar people took good care of Poc Hogan. They got him books and sent him to school. Several years later he found his family. That was good for his heart—and his soul.

Down on the Farm

Fast-forward to 1987. Here we were at Poc Hogan's farmhouse. It was similar to the old wartime houses, except it had a tin roof instead of a straw roof. It also had electricity, a refrigerator, and a television set. Significantly, a new concrete road went by the house.

We sat on the floor on cushions in front of a long table covered with multicolored food. We only ate what we were familiar with. It was very good, especially when we washed it down with plenty of *Soju*, which is the Korean equivalent of our vodka.

It was a day to remember. Many stores were told. It was hard to believe that this was taking place and we were part of it. It was a war story with a happy ending. The adventures Poc Hogan had and his finding his family at last would make a fine novel, partly because the details were beyond belief.

Come to think of it, so were the details of my short time in Korea that I spent "running with the dogs."

Appendix A
Massacre at Hoengsong
By Gary Turbak

The grisly scene, horrible almost beyond belief, shocked even the toughest men of the 7th Marine Regiment. Some averted their eyes. Others broke off their macho banter to talk in hushed, church-line tones. It was death that spooked them—death that hung like an eerie cloud over the narrow valley north of Hoengsong, Korea, that cold, quiet day in 1951.

In early February, with the Chinese offensive stalled, U.N. commanders prepared a counter assault across the center of the Korean peninsula. This time, however, Republic of Korea (ROK) troops were to do the bulk of the fighting—with elements of various U.S. infantry, artillery and other units supporting them. The notion of Americans supporting ROK troops was very much an experiment—one U.S. military leaders later regretted.

What U.N. commanders didn't know was that Communist forces also were launching a major offensive and had moved four Chinese and two North Korean divisions into the area north of the village of Hoengsong. On February 11, ROKs tangled with Communist forces, quickly disintegrating the planned South Korean offensive.

At one point, GIs of the supporting 15th Field Artillery (FA) Battalion (2nd Division) encamped for the night, relying on ROK infantry for protection. When the Chinese attacked in the dark, the South Koreans fled. The enemy swarmed over the U.S. position. Some 204 artillerymen ultimately died, resulting in one of the most concentrated losses of American lives in the entire war, according to Joseph Gould in *Korea: The Untold Story.*

Retreating ROKs streamed south past U.S. support forces, allowing the Chinese to flank American positions. Soon, the Chinese owned the narrow, twisting valley north of Hoengsong and the road that ran through it—the only escape route.

Steep hills rose up on both sides of the road, turning the valley into a shooting gallery. The Chinese relentlessly rained mortar fire down on the withdrawing and vastly outnumbered GIs. Later came the hand-to-hand fighting.

"At times," said one battalion commander, "U.N. troops lined up on one side of the road and tossed grenades at the enemy attacking from the other side of the road."

Fighting Withdrawal

During one withdrawal, forward observer (for the mortar platoon) Sgt. Charles Long of M Company, 38th Infantry Regiment, 2nd Division, chose to remain at his position atop Hill 300. It was rapidly being overrun, so he wanted to better direct mortar fire on the Chinese. For a while, he held off the enemy with rifle fire and grenades, but his last radio message reported that he was out of ammo. He used his last words to call for 40 rounds of high explosive fire on his own position, by that time swarming with enemy soldiers. For his bravery, Long posthumously received the Medal of Honor.

American rescue forces fought their way north from Hoengsong to the besieged units only to find that a river of Chinese soldiers poured in behind them. Points secured just an hour or so earlier reverted quickly to enemy hands.

U.S. infantrymen tried to clear an escape route for the howitzers, supply trucks and other vehicles, but Chinese soldiers were everywhere. U.S. artillery fired point blank into ranks of attacking enemy, but it did little good.

As soon as the withdrawing GIs pushed through one Chinese strongpoint, they would run smack into another—while enemy forces re-formed behind them. Some 2,000 Chinese troops manned one enormous roadblock. But the route south was the only way out. So the Americans continued to run this meat grinder of a gauntlet toward Hoengsong, taking heavy losses all the way.

Finally, the column of weary survivors reached Hoengsong. GIs who made it to the village joined a more general and less hazardous retreat farther south and lived to fight another day. Yet in the little valley to the north there was only death.

Enormous Graveyards

On March 7th, the 7th Marines re-entered the area north of Hoengsong for the first time since the rout three weeks earlier. Frozen in time—and frozen literally—the battle scene remained eerily preserved.

"Everyone looked into the valley and saw the smoke twisting toward the sky," wrote Marine Bill Merrick in his book *Tan Vat*. "The smoke came from overturned trucks and jeeps. They had burned so long only the frames remained.

The area looked like an enormous graveyard with the bodies unburied. The troops lay in the road, in the rice paddies, and in the cabs of the trucks that had not caught on fire."

Hundreds of GI bodies remained where they had fallen. "We had to push arms, legs, and heads to the side of the road so vehicles behind us would not run over dead soldiers," wrote Marine Rod Bennett. Some GIs had been stripped naked by enemy soldiers. One naked, dead soldier lay across the barrel of an anti-tank gun. In many trucks, dead Americans lay behind the wheel or hung out the doors. One truck contained two lifeless GIs and two dead Chinese soldiers.

"The road was blocked by a Sherman tank with one set of tracks blown off," wrote Merrick. "The hatch was open and the tank commander was hanging out of it. His jacket was full of holes, and blood made a big design on his back. Two GIs with their hands tied behind them had been shot in the back of the head. There were powder burns on the back of the caps they wore."

Marines, sickened by the sight, erected a sign along the body-strewn road. It read: "Massacre Valley, Scene of Harry S. Truman's Police Action. Nice Going, Harry!"

U.S. units suffering losses in the Hoengsong debacle included elements of the 38th and 17th Infantry; 15th, 503rd, 49th, 96th and 674th Field Artillery Battalions; 82nd Antiaircraft Artillery Automatic Weapons Battalion; and the 187th Airborne RCT.

Several outfits incurred severe battle deaths. Korean War vet Dick Ecker, using the Army's Adjutant General's Korean War Casualty File, determined the following breakdown by unit:

15th Field Artillery Battalion—208 (106 KIA & 102 in captivity)

503rd Field Artillery Battalion—56 (27 KIA & 39 in captivity)

38th Infantry Regiment—462 (328 KIA & 134 perished in captivity)

Among the 15th's dead was its commander, Lt. Col. John Keith, and MSgt. Jimmie Holloway, both of whom died after being taken prisoner. Holloway was recommended for the Medal of Honor, but it was downgraded to the Distinguished Service Cross, according to the 15th historian, Dan Gillotti.

Ecker summed it up succinctly: "It was, of course, the nature of the fatalities in this action that was the real tragedy—many of them MIA, never found and declared dead or captured and died in captivity."

Because military authorities tried to hide the extent of the disaster, casualty figures regarding the Hoengsong massacre are extremely jumbled. But according to a *Time* war correspondent, "It was part of the most horribly concentrated display of American dead since the Korean War began."

From Changbong-ni to Hoengsong

Paul G. McCoy was a member of the 82nd AAA, B Battery, serving in Korea at the time of the massacre at Hoengsong. His account of what he saw and experienced appears on The Patriot Files website and is reprinted below:

On 11 February, prior to midnight, we received word that the 8th ROK Division was under severe attack by Chinese forces. This soon turned into a collapse of the ROK units, and SF-21 started a delayed effort to load vehicles and attempt our own withdrawal. Our delay was caused by the complete loss of communications with the ROK unit we were supporting and a lack of control of SF-21 by US Forces. Our withdrawal did not start until 0200 hours, 12 February. By this time, the Changbong-ni area was inundated with fleeing ROK forces being closely followed by elements of several Chinese divisions.

By the time our column started its withdrawal, it came under sporadic machine gun fire and, as the intensity of the fire increased, the movement of the column became more disparate. At this time, I was ranked out of the front seat of my jeep by Captain Joyce, who was acting as assistant to Captain Stevens, our Commanding Officer. As we were not moving, I left the jeep to move up the column to find out what was wrong. I was not certain that my actions were particularly brave, but it certainly saved my life and provided me with knowledge as to how soldiers can act when they are completely uninformed.

As I moved up the line of vehicles, I discovered that there would be a group of 5-10 vehicles with a huge gap between the lead vehicle and the rest of the column. Each lead vehicle did not have a person in the driver's seat. It wasn't that these drivers had been killed in their vehicle, for they had apparently abandoned their vehicles.

My mission became a task of finding drivers to get that portion of the column moving. In one case, I found 10-15 men huddled in the rear of a truck as if the canvas top would provide protection from the rapidly increasing enemy fire. I asked them if anyone could drive and one soldier admitted he could, but didn't have a driver's license. I broke normal military procedure in order to get the column moving. I estimate that 10 percent of the vehicles in that column were without drivers and were blocking the road at a time when rapid movement would have placed them a long way down the road to Hoengsong and safety.

I finally worked my way past an M-16 which was the third

vehicle in the column, and climbed on the rear deck of a tank which was not moving. The tank commander told me that he was stopped because the Lieutenant in the leading vehicle was stopping every time the tank fired its cannon. The next time the lead tank stopped, I climbed onto its rear deck and discovered that it had no commander—the gunner reported that the Lieutenant had abandoned his tank. I gave orders that they were to shoot and scoot at the same time, and not stop scooting until I ordered them to do so.

About a mile down the road, just south of Nongoi, we had outrun the enemy fire, and I directed the lead tank off the road and advised the sergeant, now tank commander, to take the lead as soon as the rest of the column caught up with us. We waited for 10 minutes, and no one came up to join us. I then ordered the sergeant to take the lead and head down the road toward Hoengsong. I stood on the rear deck of the second tank with intentions of jumping off when we reached the first US unit so I could report what was happening.

As we approached the bridge north of Haktam-ni, the steep side of hill 310 was on the left of the narrow road, and a deep gorge with a small stream was on the right. The lead tank was hit with a burst of machine gun fire from a Chinese roadblock at the bridge. The tank pulled to its left into the steep side of hill 310. The tank I was on attempted to pull around the halted tank which had every possible gun firing. As we came beside the tank, ours was hit with a rocket launcher missile. I was blown off the vehicle and inside that tank all the crew had been killed. Two survivors from the first tank joined me on the road behind the two knocked-out vehicles which now completely blocked the road approach to the bridge.

We three survivors dropped down into the gorge on the

left side of the road, and headed south, parallel to the road toward Haktam-ni. We attempted three times to cross the road onto more level terrain but each time we ran into enemy forces. Finally, just north of the bridge, we ran up against a cliff which we could not climb. Again, we made a very cautious attempt to cross to the east side, but just short of the road we stopped and must have spent 10 minutes trying to figure out what a small glowing red light on the road meant to our survival. When we got near enough we discovered it was an abandoned jeep with a large radio which had not been turned off. We quickly moved across the road and started crossing the river between hills 206 and 333. When we reached the middle of the river, flares started popping over our heads. It was difficult to keep the other two men from moving while the flares were glowing.

Once on the other side of the river, we made our way to the east of hill 206, then south towards the road from Saemal. In the process, we turned the flank of an infantry company from the 3rd Battalion of the 38th Infantry, which was guarding Saemal. After a short and terrifying period of proving that we were not Chinese, we were escorted to the Battalion HQ where I reported what happened. At this point, nothing I had seen indicated a massive Chinese attack, and I could not understand why the Battalion would not immediately go to the rescue of SF-21. At this time I was informed that the road between Saemal and Hoengsong had been cut off. This information and what I had seen made me realize how critical the situation had become.

Stragglers from SF-21 started arriving about mid-morning of 12 February. I found out that D Battery now consisted of only 25 or so men, and not more than 4 or 5 of its M-16s were in operating condition. At the same time, the perimeter came under very heavy attack. About noon we started a breakout with an infantry company on each side of the road with the remaining M-16s providing support to the infantry.

On one point on the road, a Chinese mortar had zeroed in on a bottleneck which could not be avoided. My M-16 went through the impact area, but the vehicle behind me appeared reluctant to follow. So, I left my vehicle, counted the pop from the mortar, and attempted to encourage the commander to follow. However, I missed a pop, and a mortar round hit my left foot. My momentum was sufficient to propel me out of the impact area, and a bit of crawling into a ditch provided some protection, at least until the Chinese put a machine gun into position so as to be able to rake the ditch.

At that time, I suggested to several men around a corner and out of the line of fire behind a building, that it would be appropriate to haul the wounded around that corner. This they did and then administered a dose of morphine, loaded me into a jeep and the others into a 3/4 ton vehicle, gave me an M-1 rifle and a bandoleer of ammunition, and headed us on our way to Hoengsong. On that trip, one Chinese grenade hit the support bars for the canvas top of my jeep—I watched it explode beside the rear wheel and then thanked God that it was only a concussion grenade. On the left side of the vehicle, an enemy soldier with a burp gun started firing at us.

With only my M-1 in a jeep with a rapidly shattering windshield, I could only aim with the front of the muzzle in front of the driver's nose and wait until the jeep moved into a position so I could fire at the enemy. The last round he fired went across the driver's belly, and passed through the upper portion of my thigh. At this point, I was perched on the small fender outside the jeep, my right leg was still in good shape, when another bullet passed through my calf, then between the driver and myself, while I continued hanging on.

Soon the driver saw an M-16 ahead which was lumbering down the center of the road. The road had a sharp drop-off into the rice paddies on each side. After I asked if he thought he could pass around the M-16, we decided that the enemy fire was so heavy that we had no choice but to try. With the morphine slowing my reflexes, I did not draw my right leg into the jeep before my foot hit the rear of the M-16. The impact broke my right ankle.

My memory of what happened after that is not too reliable, but both vehicles made it into Hoengsong. Furthermore, after reading such phrases as "massacre valley," I gather that the carnage just north of Hoengsong was worse than that of the initial attack on SF-231. If so, the retreat from Saemal must have been a horrible example of a command failure by X-Corps.

Many of my comrades in SF-21 were the unfortunate who died under the control of an inept ROK command structure and without access to US support and control. As some contemporary US Senators might say, "Shame on you, General Almond."

I remain one of the fortunate soldiers of SF-21.

Historian/Vietnam veteran Gary Turbak was a freelance writer based in Missoula, Montana, until his untimely death on August 21, 2004.

Reprinted with permission from *Battles of the Korean War: Americans Engage in Deadly Combat, 1950–1953*, editor Richard K. Kolb (Kansas City, MO: Veterans of Foreign Wars, 2010, 2nd ed., 46–47).

Appendix B
Angel of the Marines
A Story of the Ultimate Sacrifice in a War Long Forgotten
By Fred E. Kasper, USN

Steam glistened hints of gray and blue as it spiraled over the roadways and rooftops in the quaint little town of Taunton, Massachusetts. It was early spring 1944 as the morning frost invitingly greeted the sun. The smell of fresh baked bread filled the air for blocks, tantalizing the senses of even the strongest willed. At the corner nickel and dime store, the shop owner carefully swept dirt from the sidewalk with a cornhusk broom and hurriedly opened his doors for the day's activities. American flags gently waved in testament of proud display from several storefronts, while fueled debate over the war echoed from the local barbershop. Down the road the paperboy made his exchange to passing motorists on their way to work: "Extra ... Extra ... Read all about it ... get your *Daily Gazette* here ... Three cents!"

Further along town, Richard DeWert, a quiet and playful

13-year-old, meticulously built a makeshift fort out of cardboard in his backyard. Pretending to be a doctor, he carefully bandaged the injuries of his make-believe comrades and conjured visions of these toy soldiers winning the war against the axis powers in Europe. His imagination was oftentimes the only refuge he had in the turmoil and confusion he called home. Richard's natural mother continuously struggled to care for him as a single mother; however, with mounting pressures, she lost the battle to her own demons and regretfully had to place him in a foster home.

Richard now faced a serious dilemma at a very young age, one of substantial pain and sorrow, as loneliness shattered his playful spirit and forced him to grow old beyond his years. His loneliness was quickly answered when Albertina and Joseph Roy welcomed Richard into their home. The Roys were unable to have children to call their own and were tormented by this grim reality. Richard quickly became the child the Roys never had and flourished in the love and comfort they provided to him, so much, in fact, that he began to dream of the future for the first time. His dream was to join the Navy and become a doctor.

He excitedly shared this dream with anyone that would listen, especially the Roys, who offered him the valuable encouragement he needed. A compassionate young man was quickly developing. This compassion was further highlighted some years later when Richard went on a chaperoned date with a local girl and witnessed a small dog in the middle of the road. The dog was near starvation and in miserable condition, shivering uncontrollably from the cold and rain. Richard pleaded for them to stop the vehicle as he gently picked up the dog and returned to the car. He then brought the animal home and spent the next several days nurturing it back to full health.

How this spirited little boy who saved a small dog developed into one of America's greatest heroes will be left for all readers to ponder. What is known is how Richard DeWert consistently displayed acts of selflessness and compassion in the approaching years that touched the lives of an entire nation, and captured the hearts and minds of every Marine, Sailor, Soldier, and Airman. A hero, as you will read, deeply committed to his country, and befitting of his nation's highest military award, the Medal of Honor.

As 1945 came to a close, the news of victory in World War II was still unfolding. Our troops were finally coming home and a sense of tranquility gradually resumed in this small town. An average student, Richard was frequently preoccupied and never quite satisfied with his place in the classroom. A burning passion resided within him outside of school, a passion that somehow knew there were bigger things in store for him. As the months went by, Richard took up a job at a local butcher shop for extra spending money; however, his dream to serve his country and one day become a doctor continued to be foremost in his mind.

Soft-spoken and ambitious, he remained more determined than ever to see his dream become a reality. Having just turned 17 a month earlier, he walked in to the Navy Recruiting Station in Brockton, Massachusetts, and enlisted in the Navy as a Hospital Corpsman. The date was December 2, 1948. He would have one day to say good-bye to the Roys, for he would be shipping off to Boot Camp the following day.

From December 3, 1948, until July 22, 1949, Richard attended basic training and Hospital Corps "A" School at the Naval Training Center, Great Lakes, Illinois. In late July

1949, he received orders to the Naval Hospital, Portsmouth, Virginia, where he later applied to attend Operating Room Technician School. As events developed in the Korean Peninsula following North Korea's invasion of South Korea on June 25, 1950, the US Military responded by going on full alert. Consequently, Richard dropped out of Operating Room Technician School and volunteered to serve with the First Medical Battalion, First Marine Division.

As Richard prepared for deployment while waiting at Camp Pendleton, California, in August of 1950, he met a Dental Technician by the name of Francis J. Redding (now a retired Lieutenant Commander in the Navy's Medical Service Corps). They soon realized they had a lot in common: both were assigned to First Medical Battalion, both the rank of E-3, and both shared the same age.

They were quickly dispatched on numerous work details loading gear and equipment aboard ships in San Diego as the urgency of getting our forces to Korea grew by the minute. The little spare time they had was swiftly consumed as they received crash courses on how to properly wear their new Marine uniforms, assemble their field equipment, and make the gradual and oftentimes tough adjustment to the Marine Corps. It was unknown to them at the time just how soon their lives would change forever, as innocence turned to harsh reality and the United States fully engaged in actions against North Korea.

Richard and Francis spent the next six months together with the First Medical Battalion as they assembled field hospitals, took in the wounded, and embarked on numerous campaigns to include the amphibious assault and seizure of Inchon, South Korea; the assault and liberation of Seoul,

South Korea; and the First Marine Division's advance deep into, and the subsequent withdrawal from North Korea.

"He was a fairly reserved person, and was very gung-ho," recalled Redding, who currently resides in New York. From the very onset of operations at Inchon, Hospitalman (HN) Richard DeWert repeatedly requested to be transferred with the front-line Marines, where he felt he could be more effective. "It was the stuff heroes are made of, as if he knew his destiny, and it was written there before him," recalls Redding. It wasn't long before Richard's time with Francis and the First Medical Battalion came to an end, however, as he was ordered to the "Mighty Seventh Marines."

Upon reactivation on 17 August 1950, the Seventh Marine Regiment was called upon time and time again as a fighting machine to be reckoned with in turning the tides against the North Korean and Chinese Communist Forces. They frequently encountered insurmountable odds, and paid dearly in American lives. In the months preceding Richard's arrival, "Dog" Company, Second Battalion, Seventh Marines (D-2-7) had experienced some of the most epic small arms battles in history. In contrast, the Seventh Marine Regiment suffered more casualties than any other Marine unit in the Korean War, according to Jim Lawrence, Operations Officer for Second Battalion Seventh Marines at the time. Lawrence, a veteran of Korea and the battle for Guadalcanal in WWII, continued a successful 30-year career in the Marine Corps until his retirement in 1972 as a Brigadier General.

From the time they landed at Inchon, Dog Company faced critical challenges collectively and as individual Marines, while life and death hung in the balance at every corner. During operations in the capture of Seoul on 26 September 1950, Dog Company, having been informed that the city was secure, walked into an ambush of well-entrenched North Korean soldiers. Pinned down under intense small arms and automatic fire, the men from Dog Company put up a courageous fight, and despite heavy casualties, survived as a unit. This was their first major encounter in battle since arriving in Korea and it would turn out to be a very costly one, with nearly one quarter of their Marines killed or wounded. The bloody battle at Sudaemun Prison had ended. However, this was only the first of many wounds the men from "Dog" Company would be licking.

Five days after the battle at Sudaemun Prison, Dog Company engaged in an overwhelming victory in the battle at Uijongbu, 18 miles northeast of Seoul. They then embarked on ship again at Inchon, for their subsequent landing at Wonson, North Korea, in late October. Upon landing at Wonson, Dog Company made steady advances north to the cities of Hamhung and Sudong. It was on November second in Sudong that the 7th Marines made history by being the first Marine unit to engage the Chinese Communist Forces since the onset of the Korean War. It was a ferocious battle that inflicted over 1,500 casualties on the 124th Chinese Communist Division. A humiliating defeat that prompted the Chinese Communist Forces to take revenge in the following weeks in what would come to be known as the infamous Chosin Reservoir Campaign.

The Main Supply Route (MSR) for the First Marine Division, stretching some 78 miles from the seaport town of Hungnam to Yudam-ni, North Korea, was of critical tactical importance. Following the victory at Sudong, Dog Company, along with the Fifth Marines, made their way to the most northern tip of this supply route along the Chosin Reservoir. Unbeknown at the time, the Chinese Communist Forces were massing in unimaginable numbers for their infiltration into North Korea with one objective in mind: to completely annihilate the First Marine Division and leave no Marine alive. The Chinese Ninth Army Group, consisting of five field armies of over 120,000 troops, was the weapon of choice in accomplishing this destructive objective. Thus, the start of the Chosin Reservoir Campaign had begun.

During operations in Yudam-ni, west of the Chosin Reservoir, Dog Company set up a defensive perimeter on hill 1240 as increasing reports from patrols indicated Chinese Communist Forces were in the area. On the evening of 25 November, over 180,000 Chinese troops broke through the US Eighth Army's line to the east, while 120,000 additional Chinese troops enveloped the First Marine Division at the main supply route. As they prepared for the inevitable, Dog Company came under heavy attack just after midnight on 27 November. The men from "Dog" courageously fought for their lives and suffered incredible losses as they were forced to withdraw from the hill.

Private First Class Tom Cassis, assigned to the machine gun section, describes the events in taking hill 1240: "The temperatures were bitter cold, ranging from -30 to -40 degrees Fahrenheit. We were heavily outnumbered and began taking large numbers of dead and wounded. After getting the order to withdraw from the hill I remembered getting hit in the arm with an enemy round that hit me so hard it literally twirled me around in a circle. I must have made the world record for the 400-yard dash in shoepacks and parka after that as I finally arrived at our withdraw point at the base of the hill."

By the time Cassis made it to the aid station he would have to wait his turn to be treated, as the corpsmen were completely overwhelmed with casualties. Tom Cassis, now a retired lawyer who resides in Washington, kept the enemy .45 caliber round that passed through his canteen and caused considerable soft tissue damage to his left arm.

No sooner had they recovered from their losses and treated the wounded from hill 1240, the Marines of Dog Company were ordered to retake the hill again the following day. With an available strength of only 20 men against an enemy strength of roughly two battalions, the Marines miraculously retook the hill as reinforcements from the Fifth Marines arrived. By the time Dog Company arrived to Hungnam, North Korea, in mid-December 1950, following the Chosin Reservoir withdrawal they had suffered: 50 killed in action, 128 wounded in battle, and 50 non-battle injuries mostly from frostbite.

With the original company strength of just over 200, the men of Dog Company, Second Battalion, Seventh Marines, First Marine Division paved their way in blood as they again struggled to survive as a unit and establish themselves as a key element in the proud history of the United States Marine Corps.

The latter part of December 1950 was fairly uneventful for Dog Company as they arrived in Masan (known as the "bean patch"), just outside of Pusan, South Korea by way of ship from the Chosin area. Without an officer to lead them, only 16 enlisted men remained after their horrific ordeal on hill 1240, and subsequent withdraw from the Chosin Reservoir. While in Masan, they received new Marines from the Third and Fourth Replacement Drafts, cleaned their weapons, and conducted training. This downtime would be bittersweet, however, as they received the order to move out again in early January 1951 to the surrounding areas of Pohang, South Korea.

Operation "Gorilla Hunt," a mission to pursue trapped North Korean Soldiers from the earlier campaign in Seoul, had recently commenced. The men of Dog Company, like warrior nomads in a wasteland, would venture into unknown territory, in search of an elusive enemy. Although early encounters with the North Korean forces were reported in large numbers, only minimal contact was made in the following weeks as they made the treacherous trip north by way of truck and foot to the outskirts of H'ongch'on, South Korea. During this period, they experienced fierce artillery attacks to their positions, nearly escaped with their lives as a flash flood threatened to wash them away while they were bivouacked near a dry riverbed, and again encountered heavy enemy resistance in early March 1951.

Division Special Order #69-51, dated March 6, 1951, directed Hospital man Richard DeWert to detach from Headquarters and Service Company, First Medical Battalion, and report to Commanding Officer, Seventh Marine Regiment, for duty. Richard had finally received the news he so willingly pursued; his request to join the Marines on the front lines had been granted.

As Richard got his things in order for his arrival to Dog Company, Third Platoon, Second Battalion, Seventh Marines, his first thoughts were of those Marines he would soon be a part of as he pleaded and bartered within the First Medical Battalion to obtain extra supplies to include brand-name Band-Aids® and aspirin, a very rare commodity at this time. As the messenger of compassion and mercy, Richard mentally and physically prepared himself for the monumental task that lay ahead.

Brisk temperatures crept through the valley floor and canyon, while fog gradually gave way to patches of blue sky. Thundering artillery pounded several hillsides in the distance as reconnaissance jets passed overhead to mark enemy positions for the advancing forces on the ground. Operation "Ripper," a mission to inflict as many casualties as possible on the Chinese Communist Forces to keep them off balance and prevent a counterattack, was scheduled to kick off the following day. Meanwhile, Dog Company prepared their men for offensive maneuvers just north of Hoengsong, South Korea, at the Kunsamma Pass, when a jeep suddenly pulled up to company headquarters.

With thick brown hair, a medium build, and a baby face that permeated innocence, Richard briefly glanced around, stepped out of the jeep, and grabbed his medical bag and a large round wicker basket from the back seat. As he proceeded to the Company Command Post, he was given his field equipment, C-rations, and directions to Third Platoon, about a half mile down the road. While he made his approach to Third Platoon, weighted down by his gear and equipment, he reported in to the Platoon Commander, a First Lt. Richard Humphreys. "There he was, carrying this large wicker basket overflowing with medical gear and medications. I'm used to seeing corpsman check in with a sea-bag loaded with personal gear and other items, but not him. When I asked him how he was going to carry all of that stuff he replied, 'It's my duty, sir, I have to carry it.'"

Lt. Humphreys knew right away that he was dealing with a special breed of corpsman, "a corpsman of Marines in every way." Richard Humphreys, a Silver Star and Bronze Star with combat "V" recipient, and veteran of WWII, Korea, and Vietnam, continued a long and prestigious career in the

Marine Corps until his retirement at the rank of Colonel in 1970.

As Dog Company proceeded north, Richard DeWert quickly integrated with the third platoon as they conducted patrols and sought out enemy positions. Building rapport with his Marines and settling into a routine that consisted mostly of long marches with 85 pounds on his back, digging defensive fighting holes, and frequent medical calls to members in the platoon, oftentimes under heavy fire, Richard, like countless corpsmen before him, was intimately aware that the lives of each of his Marines was entrusted in his care. He also knew that ultimately his duty was to risk his life in order to save the lives of others. An epiphany that many battlefield corpsmen quickly come to terms with.

On March 7, one day after Richard arrived to the company, they proceeded north of Hoengsong, South Korea. It was here that the men of Dog Company witnessed horrors beyond imagination as they discovered the aftermath of a Chinese and North Korean ambush to elements of an Army Convoy. Although the onslaught had occurred 3 weeks earlier, it was a battle site eerily preserved, as bodies remained frozen where they died. Attached to this convoy were units from the US Army's 38th Infantry Regiment, 503rd Field Artillery Battalion, 15th Field Artillery Battalion, and an attachment from the Dutch Field Artillery Battalion.

"Bodies were everywhere, most of them had been stripped of their clothing and down to their underwear before being shot," stated Fred Frankville, a Private First Class and rifleman assigned to third platoon. "There were literally hundreds of bodies strewn about, some in jeeps, others with their weapons still clinched in their hands, all frozen in time. Seeing their final expressions captured on their faces, like figures in a wax museum, just didn't appear to be real at first. It was a grisly sight I and others will never forget," said Frankville.

Tom Cassis recalled his account of what he saw on this day by saying: "There were vehicles overturned and on their sides; some were still burning and giving off smoke. I remember seeing an awful lot of dead, at least 50 or 100 at first glance. What stuck in my mind the most was seeing two Chinese in front of us that had been run over by a tank; the track marks could still be seen on their backs as they were flattened to a height of maybe two inches." This area, known as "Massacre Valley," resulted in a death toll of over 700 Americans, and only one survivor for the Dutch. This was the heaviest loss for any Dutch Battalion in their long history of warfare, and the highest concentration of American dead from a single location in the Korean War.

By March 11, 1951, Dog Company moved further north of Hoengsong, while Operation "Ripper" gained momentum. They had encountered slight opposition early that morning as one Marine received a life-threatening wound to the head. Richard quickly jumped into action, stabilized the Marine, and continued with the platoon as they set up flank security and continued on small patrols. At around midnight, Third Platoon received a desperate call for help over the radio from First Platoon who was pinned down from heavy fire at the hands of Chinese aggressors.

As the Third Platoon advanced in an effort to reinforce the troubled First Platoon, Chinese grenadier's viciously attacked their position. "Explosions erupted everywhere as shrapnel pierced through the surrounding trees, hurling splinters and fragments of earth in every direction. When the smoke cleared, four Marines, including myself, were severely wounded. I counted 11 or 12 grenades thrown at us before I got hit," stated Jack Larson, a Sergeant, Rifleman, and Squad Leader assigned to third platoon at the time.

"Richard was frantic as he patched everyone up and moved through incoming fire with little regard for his own safety. That's about the time I got injured," Larson said. Although severely wounded himself and losing blood at an alarming rate, Sergeant Larson refused initial treatment, continued a ferocious fight with the enemy, and saved the company from certain destruction. He was awarded the Navy Cross, the Navy and Marine Corps' second-highest military award for his heroic actions on this day.

Running on adrenaline, Richard wouldn't have time to immediately reflect on what had just happened; while his platoon received 4 casualties, the rest of the company suffered 2 killed in action, and 7 others critically wounded. The priority for him was to evacuate the wounded and quickly get back with the platoon where he was needed.

Almost as quickly as it had started, the offensive at Hoengsong had ended. By March 15, Dog Company was placed in reserve in anticipation of getting their company back up to strength. Marines from the 6th Replacement Draft gradually filtered in during this time while much-needed supplies, and more importantly, mail call reinvigorated the spirits of the war-battered and exhausted Marines. Only sporadic encounters with the enemy were made on isolated patrols around their perimeter as they received a well-deserved break, their first break in the rear since they left the "Bean Patch" in early January.

They caught up on writing letters to friends and loved ones, recycled old magazines that must have been read by each of them at least ten times, and cooked C-Rations around squad fires while engaging in familiar conversation. Most of the dialogue consisted of the types of American foods they would sink their teeth into when they returned home, the anticipation of reunions with girlfriends, wives, and their children, and the occasional heated topic of who had the best car. Richard wouldn't have much time to relax, however, as he was busy making his rounds and treating the minor ailments that couldn't receive attention during the heat of combat and constant movements.

"Richard DeWert was a true professional and was deeply compassionate," stated Fred Frankville, recalling how Richard provided aid to him for a severe headache during their short break in the rear. "He pulled out this bottle of Bayer® aspirin and handed me a couple as he looked me over to make sure I was all right. He carried a lot of brand-name medicines in his bag of tricks, and I don't think I need to tell you just how comforting it was to receive a hint of home like that."

For those Marines who remembered Richard DeWert, his impact was far reaching, for no other corpsman they remember went the extra mile in the fashion he did. As Richard continued to care for his Marines, offering glimpses of hope and cheering up the despondent, the inseparable bond between Marine and corpsman intensified.

It wasn't long before Dog was back up to strength and on the move again. As they resumed the all-too-familiar routine of digging fighting holes, engaging in firefights with the enemy, and gaining ground, rumors began to surface throughout the company that they will soon be put under control of the Army's 1st Cavalry Division.

The 1st Cavalry Division at this time was preparing for operations south of the 38th parallel in efforts to fortify their lines and push the Chinese Communist Forces back north. "I remember when the company received a brief about how the

North Korean and Chinese Forces were massing just north of us. That's also about the time we were told that the Seventh Marines were being placed under the 1st Cavalry Division," stated Ed Garr, a Private First Class Machine Gunner from third section, assigned to the third platoon.

Garr, a veteran of Korea and Vietnam, and recipient of two Bronze Star Medals, went on to say: "Shortly after that we spotted a motorcade of jeeps in the distance, only to discover that it was the famous General MacArthur visiting our troops in the field."

While the men from Dog Company made their way north for their eventual arrival to the 1st Cavalry Division, tension and excitement began to mount with the Marines. The push north meant progress for the United Nations; a small indication that maybe this nightmare would be over soon. Covering ground that had already been covered before, and even more alarming, moving towards the 38th parallel, brought back visions of their lurid and narrow escape just months earlier in the Chosin area.

Fighting continued for Dog Company as they made their northward journey, with skirmishes and ambushes to their position at nearly every stretch of the way. "It seemed like a never-ending struggle of taking one hill after another. First we attack, then dig in, and wait for the counter-attack, only to repeat the same process for days on end," stated Gonzalo Garza, Platoon Sergeant for third platoon. "Richard DeWert was my fox-hole buddy, and let me tell you, he was always on the move providing medical aid to the platoon."

Garza recalled one day in particular as they were preparing fighting holes, the temperature was so cold you could barely penetrate the ground. Richard was going from foxhole to foxhole checking up on everybody as he gradually made it back to Garza who was shaking uncontrollably from the cold. Richard immediately took off his sweater and said "Hey, Sarge, why don't you take my sweater, I'm from Massachusetts and I'm used to the cold; you're from Texas and you're not."

Garza was deeply touched by Richard's compassion and willingness to make such sacrifices. "We talked quite a bit, mostly about our hometowns, our dreams, and aspirations. He even told me about how he saved a small dog when he was just a kid, and about how he really wanted to become a medical doctor," said Garza. Gonzalo Garza, a Bronze Star recipient, and veteran of the battle for Okinawa in WWII and Korea, pursued a long career as an educator after leaving the Marine Corps in 1953, earning his Doctorate Degree in philosophy.

By April 1st, Dog Company arrived at their objective point with the 1st Cavalry Division. They received marching orders and operations plans, replenished depleted supplies, and prepared for their move further north. Although this was only a brief break from combat before they were to move out on trucks with the Army, the Marines took full advantage of this time as they consumed hot meals, cleaned up, and caught up on some much-needed rest.

Fred Frankville chuckled as he reminisced about the events on that day. "I'll never forget the encounter Richard DeWert and I had with this Army Medic and his buddies. Out of curiosity I asked this medic why he didn't carry a weapon. The medic replied by saying that they weren't allowed to carry them. That's when I said, 'Let me show you our corpsman!' I then called Richard DeWert over.

"As Richard approached, outfitted like Rambo, with an M-1 Carbine in his hand, and grenades attached to his belt; I could see the medic's eyes quickly widen like saucers. Richard had this half-smile on his face as he and the Medic sized each other up from top to bottom. Not a single word was exchanged between them as Richard then strutted off to his position with the rest of the platoon. There's always been healthy competition among the services, and that will probably never change; seeing Richard's pride in being with us, and our pride in him on that day said a thousand words."

As Dog Company disembarked from Army vehicles on April 2, they were given the order to seize phase lines "Dover" and "Troy" in the Chunchon vicinity, just south of the 38th parallel. Once these objectives were completed they were given the additional order to proceed to an area just north of the 38th parallel to capture several hills (objectives 43, 44, and 49) occupied by the 117th Division, 39th Corps of the Chinese Communist Forces.

Richard and his platoon ventured into some of the roughest terrain yet experienced as they overcame ferocious landslides from prevailing rains, nearly impassable roads, and massive flooding. Additional dangers were encountered by the extensive use of land mines by the enemy throughout this area. As third platoon navigated through countless dangers and obstacles on April 2nd and 3rd, their luck ran out on April 4th as they made contact with the enemy and a Marine desperately struggled to hold on to life.

A loud "Boom" and accompanying shockwave violently rustled leaves on the ground. A seismic vibration simultaneously transcended through the ground near several Marines from third platoon as everyone darted for cover. Assuming they were under mortar attack, they quickly established a defensive posture and prepared for further havoc to their position. It wasn't until moments later that "Corpsman up" was relayed within the platoon, and Richard began to edge and crawl his way closer to the wounded. Incoming rounds whizzed overhead, sending a distinctive "snap" and "crack" as they hit several trees.

Nearby, Private First Class Charles Whatley lay helpless, screaming in agony, and bleeding profusely from a blast sustained by tripping a land mine. Sergeant Garza was within feet of PFC Whatley when the tragic event occurred. "What was left of his leg was a mess as he cried out in pain. I don't know what was worse for him, the pain of being wounded or his concern for playing baseball again. Garza tried to console him and tell him he was going to be alright, but I could tell that he was badly hit."

As Richard inched forward, he carefully removed a large bandage from his bag, opened it with his teeth, and applied pressure to the mangled and nearly severed leg of Whatley. Trying desperately to ease the pain and stop the bleeding, Richard applied a tourniquet to PFC Whatley's upper thigh, administered morphine, and continued treating him for extensive shock.

While Richard continued his lifesaving attempt, the Marines effectively returned fire and cleared the area of the retreating enemy. Within an hour, the platoon established a landing zone as a helicopter swiftly evacuated their wounded comrade. Although shaken by their encounter, third platoon continued their objective for that day, marching for several more hours until they eventually traversed within feet of the 38th parallel.

Darkness swiftly approached on April 4th as Dog Company set up camp for the evening. Like a well-rehearsed orchestra, the semi synchronized "cling" and "thud" from digging against rock and difficult ground echoed along their position. Only after the foxholes were finished and the defensive perimeter established was the infamous 50 percent watch set. Some got a chance to sleep, while others scrounged what they could to eat.

Richard uneasily stirred as he tried to clear his mind of the days' events. Unable to sleep, he conducted visits to each foxhole; and with the care of a parent tucking a child in for the night, he offered reassuring encouragement and friendly conversation to each of his Marines. As he later retired into his own sleeping bag for the evening, comforted by his thoughts and efforts at being a source of strength to his brothers, he instantly fell asleep. A peaceful and sound slumber, as Richard's final hours slowly ticked away.

Dense fog tightly blanketed the ground as it slowly captured hints of first daylight. Richard, awakened by the sound of voices, sat up, rubbed his eyes, and took in his surroundings. With visibility limited to just a few feet, he quickly glanced around and blinked in succession from the cold mist deflecting off his face. As he wiped moisture from his watch and moved it back and forth to catch a glimpse of the time, he could see that it was just past five thirty in the morning.

"Everybody up and on your feet; we're moving out in one hour," came a voice from behind him. Richard slowly stood up, stretched, and took in a wide yawn. The aroma of instant coffee and burning pinecones could be detected as the sound of mess gear clattered a short distance away. He then put on his boots, drank from his canteen, and assembled his equipment for their movement out. As he looked over to Sergeant Garza who was also busy preparing his gear, he asked him, "Sarge, do you wonder if we'll ever make it out of here?"

By 0630 Dog Company and sister unit Easy Company,

Second Battalion, Seventh Marines, set off on foot, with heavy tanks in support for their joint mission in seizing objective point 43. Within an hour they crossed the 38th parallel and entered North Korea for the first time since their hasty departure in December. Temperatures gradually increased as fog slowly lifted from much of the valley floor. As the Marines continued north, their positions came under heavy attack from 60-millimeter mortar shells. Round after round poured down on their positions as they took cover and attempted to direct returning fire to the enemy.

Within minutes, the enemy pulled back and disappeared in to the distance, leaving a wake of confusion from their attack. With damage to some tanks and equipment, and minimal casualties, the Marines quickly recovered and regrouped for their advance to objective 43, an unassuming hill stretching some 439 feet high. A hill blanketed with thick vegetation, sharp inclines, and treacherous ledges. What the Marines didn't know at this time was how well-organized, pre-battle defensive bunkers were emplaced near the top of this hill; and how the Chinese lay in wait for the Marines' arrival.

A major offensive, the Seventh Marine Regiment, under the 1st Cavalry Division, had units on the attack on seven different hills (objectives 43 through 49) throughout a three-and-a-half-mile radius. While fighter jets screamed overhead, dropping their deadly cargo of Napalm, 500-pound bombs, and rockets to positions east and north of objective 43, Dog and Easy Companies slowly made their ascent up the hill. Finding two narrow fingers that paralleled one another, Dog Company took the finger to the South, while Easy Company took the finger to the west at about 9 a.m. Within visual and shouting distance from each other, Dog and Easy made steady progress in their ascent up these two natural fingers in the mountain.

After nearly an hour of climbing through patchy fog, Easy and Dog Company arrived to a clearing about three quarters of the way up when Easy Company began taking fire. A bunker containing two machine gun positions was cleverly emplaced in the middle of both fingers, enabling the Chinese to fire on both flanks at the same time. Hearing that Easy Company was under fire, Dog Company, third platoon, increased their pace as they traversed a steep ledge about 20 feet wide and to the east of Easy Company. Suddenly and without warning, third platoon began taking machine gun fire from the same enemy bunker. "The platoon was trapped under a ledge as machine gun fire opened up from above. Those that were on point and went into the clearing were the ones that got hit with enemy fire," stated Fred Frankville.

As three Marines on point position from third platoon lay severely wounded, one after each other, Richard shifted his medical gear to his side and prepared for his dash out to those in need. Aware of Richard's intentions, Sergeant Garza grabbed Richard by the arm and said, "Doc, don't go out there, wait until it's time, wait until it's clear!" Richard, on the other hand, tormented by the fate of his wounded Marines, looked at Sergeant Garza, and said, "You do your job, and I'll do mine," and quickly moved into the open against a barrage of incoming fire.

As bullets kicked up dirt in front of him, Richard dove for the ground as he arrived at the position of Private First Class Anthony Falatach, a rifleman from third platoon. Richard grabbed him by the armpits, positioned him between his legs, and kicked his way to safety as he maneuvered around on his backside. Exhausted and out of breath, Richard was hit in the leg by a blast of enemy fire just as he made it to cover with his wounded Marine.

Despite excruciating pain to his leg, Richard looked up and saw that another Marine also lay critically wounded and in need of help. As Richard dodged through a hail of machine gun fire for the second time he quickly arrived to the location of Corporal Donald Sly, grabbed him by the collar, and swiftly dragged him to safety.

With no time to rest, Richard made yet another daring rescue attempt as he crawled and slithered to the position of Private First Class Richard Durham, a rifleman from third platoon. As Richard made his approach to his helpless comrade, he received a devastating wound to his right shoulder by an enemy bullet, ripping through his flesh and shattering his bones. With rapid blood loss, and under intense pain, Richard continued moving toward PFC Durham's position, only to realize that he had been shot through the head and killed instantly. Undaunted by his own condition, Richard pulled PFC Durham's body out of the line of fire.

Unaware that an additional enemy bunker containing numerous Chinese infantrymen was located just above the machine-gun bunker, third platoon began taking sporadic fire from several snipers and sharpshooters above their position. Corporal Keith Ester, a rifleman and squad leader for third squad, was positioned to the right of his men when he was shot through the knee by a Chinese Sniper. Richard, in agony and with tear-filled eyes, looked over to Corporal Ester as he watched him fall to the ground about 15 yards away. Weak from blood loss, and refusing to submit to aid for his own wounds, Richard mustered up all the strength he could for his final selfless act.

Fred Frankville witnessed Richard's final actions, and

describes the events on that day: "It was pretty foggy as we made our way up the hill. As I advanced up the line and got a clear field of vision, the fog all of a sudden lifted, almost like a dream. That was when I saw Richard DeWert run out to Corporal Ester. As Richard leaned over him to provide aid he was mortally wounded by a burst of enemy machine gun fire and fell lifeless on top of Corporal Ester."

Having seen the tragic death of his corpsman, and realizing that Corporal Ester was still alive, Fred Frankville instinctively navigated his way to the right flank and out of the field of fire from the machine gun bunker. He then made a daring sprint towards the bunker, pointed the muzzle of his M-1 Garand through the opening and fired a full clip of 8 rounds at point-blank range, neutralizing the enemy.

After suppressing the enemy, Frankville pulled Keith Ester behind a ledge and into safety. "Seeing Richard DeWert's bravery and selfless actions was the turning point because it inspired us to move against the enemy regardless of the odds. Who knows what would have happened to us if Richard DeWert had not gone out there and did what he did; we were pinned down and clearly at the mercy of the Chinese aggressors," stated Frankville.

Shortly afterwards, Easy Company radioed their thanks to Dog Company for saving their hides, as they were helplessly pinned down as well. PFC Frankville was awarded the Silver Star for his actions during this battle; however, he and others from third platoon were compelled to give their accounts of Richard's heroic actions to others in hopes that he would be recognized for his gallant bravery and the ultimate sacrifice so freely given.

As Private First Class Chuck Curley and Corporal Art Rudd carried Richard DeWert's bloody body off the hill, it was a solemn time of reflection and awe at how one man possessed such bravery, courage, compassion, and willingness to sacrifice himself for others. As water sprayed out of Richard's canteen on their way down from the numerous bullet holes, the men of Dog Company paid respect to their fallen corpsman, as many rendered a salute and farewell to their corpsman. Sergeant Gonzalo Garza had this to say as we closed out his interview recently: "You know, I never lost one single person from my platoon from mid-February until that tragic day on April 5th. I am honored to have been by Richard's side for so many days, and equally honored to have called him 'Doc.'"

Corporal Keith Ester was the only wounded member Richard DeWert risked his life to save that actually lived to tell about it. In a recent interview with Keith Ester, he commented on Richard DeWert: "He was a very nice kid, although we didn't talk a whole lot, and he wasn't with the company for very long. It was obvious that he really cared about his duty and those around him. The Corpsman has always been a central figure with the Marine Corps, hearing that Richard DeWert was so appropriately honored after his death brought both closure and a great deal of satisfaction to many of us." Keith Ester a retired teacher and school administrator out of Denver, Colorado. Has since passed away.

One day after Richard DeWert's untimely death, third platoon received a new platoon commander, Second Lt. Lealon Wimpee, while Dog Company also received a new Company Commander, Captain Alvin Mackin. As PFC Frankville and other members from third platoon approached Lt. Wimpee and Captain Mackin and provided detailed accounts of Richard DeWert's extraordinary heroism, it became clear and obvious to them that it was most worthy of writing up and submitting for the nation's highest military award, the Medal of Honor.

Later that next year, Richard David DeWert was posthumously awarded the Medal of Honor, signed by President Harry S. Truman. On November 19, 1983, the Guided Missile Frigate USS *DeWert* (FFG 45) was christened in Bath, Maine, and was the first ship to bear his name. Richard DeWert is also a common household name in Taunton, Massachusetts, as streets, a library, a VFW hall, and even a housing development proudly shared his name.

Most recently, in 2004, two Naval Medical Clinics, one at Newport, Rhode Island, and another at the Marine Corps Mountain Warfare Training Center in Bridgeport, California, held dedication ceremonies and re-named their facilities in honor of Richard DeWert.

You can learn a lot from the horrors of war. From those that endured it, and those that gave the ultimate sacrifice. About compassion, emotion, sadness and loss. About triumph, determination, bravery, and sorrow. About just how precious life is—the priceless gift that it is, and the ultimate expression of love and human kindness in giving that life so that others may live. One can't help but wonder in amazement at the heroic actions of Hospitalman Richard DeWert, a lonely kid full of dreams from Taunton, Massachusetts.

His legacy lives on in each American today, a testament in the cost for freedom and our continued way of life. I am moved by those Marines that served with Richard DeWert; with heroes abound, Dog Company was a unique band of brothers that to this day maintains close ties among its members. Without the persistence of Marines like Fred Frankville, Lealon Wimpee, and Alvin Mackin in seeing that Richard was appropriately recognized and honored for his selfless actions, this story wouldn't have been possible. There is no greater gift than to lay down your life for your fellow man. Richard DeWert gave the ultimate sacrifice and paid the ultimate price for his country and the Marines he served with.

It has been my distinct honor to put into words the human condition shared by Richard and his Marines. To paint a picture of those that lived, cried, fought, and died in a war long forgotten. My hat is off to all Americans that have risked their lives in the name of freedom and democracy around the globe. It is with great humility and respect that I end this story by leaving you with a letter from Mrs. Albertina Roy addressed to Captain Alvin Mackin on August 9, 1951, following Richard DeWert's untimely death.

Dear Captain Mackin,

> Receiving your letter was most comforting. Knowing that Richard died so honorably eases, somewhat, the pain that will always remain in our hearts. Although we are not his natural parents, being childless, we loved him more than words can describe. He was brought up under atrocious conditions, by a mother who was only concerned about herself.
>
> Richard had to find out for himself from earliest childhood. He could have gone just as bad as he was good, but God in his infinite wisdom gave him a pure heart. He came to us, we thought at the time, quite by accident, but now we know different. God sent him to us so that we could shower him with the love and affection that he never received in early childhood, and he in turn returned that love and affection on us, that we also never received from a child of our own.

We were never able to adopt him legally as his mother would never relinquish him. His and our big aim in life was for him to become twenty-one, so that we could adopt him legally. It was not his will that it be so; however we will never forget Richard's memory and will always carry it in our hearts. Knowing that you are burdened with many and tedious duties, we thank you from the bottom of our hearts for taking the time to write us such a comforting letter.

Respectfully yours,

Mrs. Albertina Roy

Fred Kasper is a senior chief corpsman in the United States Navy. He has been in the service for over twenty-one years, with thirteen of those years serving with Marine Corps units as their "Doc." (Every corpsman is known as "Doc" to the marines he serves.) Some highlights of his career include serving on two presidential POW/MIA recovery missions to Vietnam and North Korea, and more recently, a one-year tour in Iraq. An aspiring writer, he hopes to complete a book on Richard DeWert and Dog Company 2/7 in the next year. In April 2009 Fred Kasper was promoted to master chief petty officer, the highest enlisted rank in the US Navy.

Appendix C
Dog Seventh Marine Casualties

About 1,700 marines served in Dog Company Seventh Marines from August 1950 to July 1953. The following statistics show the magnitude of their contributions to the Korean War.

- 156 killed in action
- 16 died of wounds
- 17 missing in action (3 returned as POWs as war ended)
- 942 wounded who received one Purple Heart
- 156 wounded who received two Purple Hearts
- 21 wounded who received three Purple Hearts
- 1 Medal of Honor recipient
- 5 Navy Cross recipients
- 33 Silver Star recipients
- 27 Bronze Star recipients
- 19 Letters of Commendation

Table of KIA/Died of wounds—D Co. 2nd Bn. Seventh Marines

Name	Date
Adams, John E. PFC	9/28/50
Albert, Henry J. Jr. PFC	12/8/50
Bannantine, James W. 2 LT	7/14/50
Bateman, Leroy R. PFC	12/9/51
Bigden, Jack B. SGT	11/3/50
Bosch, Edward R. PFC	5/31/52
Bruce, John F. PFC	12/8/51
Bryant, Floyd G. PFC	12/24/50
Caldwell, Ernest T. PFC	11/27/50
Colegate, David T. PFC	2/10/52
Collins, Edmund Jr. PFC	11/29/50
Cramer, Glenn R. PVT	11/27/50
Crow, Harold M. PFC	3/11/51
Damon, Robert V. SGT	4/10/51
Desrosier, John A. SGT	9/28/50
DeWert, Richard HN3	4/5/51
Dewitt, John F. SGT	3/2/51
Didonna, John PVT	1/13/51
Diemer, John W. PFC	12/1/50
Dolan, Michael J. PVT	11/28/50
Dorn, Conrad E. PVT	11/28/50
Doucette, Vernon J. PFC	11/29/50
Druzianich, John G. PFC	3/2/51
Duhr, Kenneth R. CPL	11/28/50
Dunlap, Albert H. Jr. SGT	6/11/51

Durham, Richard W. PVT	4/5/51
Eichschlag, Donald T. PVT	11/28/50
Eismin, Leonard D. PFC	7/18/52
Epp, William C. PFC	11/27/50
Fairchild, Ray P. PFC	11/27/50
Falatch, Anthony J. PFC	4/5/51
Farley, Louis G. PFC	12/1/50
Fischer, Ralph R. CPL	3/2/51
Flores, Roque I. PVT	11/28/50
Flynn, Walter M. CPL	11/28/50
Forrester, Edsel G. PFC	11/29/50
Gentry, John S. PFC	11/28/50
Griswold, Harry E. PFC	9/28/50
Gross, Lawrence L. SGT	11/27/50
Handing, Richard J. CPL	1/13/53
Hardin, William G. CPL	11/3/50
Harris, Richard E. SGT	9/26/50
Hendrix, Thomas C. SGT	6/15/52
Henry, Elton T. SGT	11/30/50
Hermosillo, Carlos PFC	5/27/51
Hill, James M. PFC	9/11/52
Hoiles, William H. PFC	3/2/51
Icett, Harold W. Jr. PFC	9/12/51
Jiminez, Manuel PFC	7/5/53
Joachinson, Edward R. K. PFC	11/28/50
Johnston, Harold M. PFC	7/24/52
Jonas, Bernard C. PFC	6/17/51
Justice, Herbert PFC	1/13/53
Kemp, Harvey D. PFC	10/27/51

Kipp, Kenneth R. SGT	12/6/50
Knott, Walter D. PFC	11/27/50
Korte, Joel PFC	11/27/50
Lease, Gene H. PFC	9/26/50
Lenoir, Edward A. HM3	3/2/51
Leonard, Reuben PVT	4/9/53
Ley, Frederick A. CPL	11/29/50
Luckenbill, Ray F. PFC	9/28/50
Mallet, Robert A. PFC	11/25/50
Mandich, Robert S. CPL	12/1/50
Matusowski, Robert J. PFC	11/28/50
McDonald, Alton C. SGT	11/30/50
McKenna, Joseph A. PFC	9/13/51
Melbye, Roland J. PFC	9/12/51
Migala, Jerome P. PVT	11/27/50
Mock, Robert C. Jr. CPL	9/29/50
Monroe, Tracy W. Jr. PFC	11/28/50
Neustadt, Alvin PFC	9/26/50
O'Neill, John SSGT	9/26/50
Padgett, William A. CPL	11/27/50
Partin, Dean W. PFC	4/25/53
Pearson, William A. CPL	11/28/50
Pieper, Rolly L. CPL	10/27/52
Pitts, Clyde T. SGT	12/6/50
Pryzgoda, Dennis A. Jr. SGT	7/20/53
Purcell, William P. TSGT	11/30/53
Rapp, Paul M. PFC	5/20/52
Rister, Harst PFC	6/15/52
Riviello, Frank V. PFC	3/2/51

Roderick, Earl F. PFC	9/30/52
Rooney, Robert F. PFC	10/27/52
Roos, Jerry M. SGT	7/21/53
Ruddle, Bobby J. SGT	4/19/53
Russell, William R. PFC	11/28/50
Schmidt, Walter S. SGT	2/08/54
Schneider, Edward C. PFC	11/28/50
Schupbach, Ward PFC	9/12/51
Sharpe, Robert V. PFC	11/30/50
Shenk, Frederick B. CPL	2/10/52
Shoemaker, Edward L. PFC	7/17/52
Shropshire, Arthur J. 1 LT	9/29/50
Sikes, Jackie P. PFC	11/28/50
Skeen, Kenneth L. PFC	7/20/53
Sly, Donald CPL	4/5/51
Smith, Douglas E. PFC	1/29/53
Smith, Herbert L. PFC	9/29/50
Smith, John B. CPL	3/28/53
Somsky, John E. Jr. CPL	3/28/53
Speaker, Thomas B. CPL	2/27/52
Stefanak, John C. PFC	4/9/53
Stewart, Charles F. HM3	12/6/50
Stewart, Joseph E. SGT	12/1/50
Stiles, Paul G. PFC	7/20/53
Stiles, Vernon L. PFC	1/13/53
Stone, Marion H. PFC	4/5/53
Talarico, John C. PFC	7/26/53
Thevenet, Delmar L. OFC	11/28/50
Thompson, Franklin B. PFC	9/28/50

Thomson, Thomas L. 1 LT	11/28/50
Tovar, Julian T. PFC	3/11/51
Vallejo, David T. PFC	8/7/53
Velasquez, Angelo M. PFC	5/27/51
Vick, John S. CPL	12/8/51
Vines, Thomas F. Jr. PFC	10/22/51
Violette, Robert J. CPL	11/28/50
Wade, Freeman N. CPL	11/27/50
Watkins, George R. PFC	1/19/52
Watt, Thomas F. CPL	4/25/53
Weber, Albert G. CPL	9/29/50
Welch, Willard M. PFC	2/7/53
Wensley, Robert G. PFC	10/11/51
Whalin, Granvil R. SGT	10/16/52
Whatley, Charles W. PFC	4/12/51
Wilcox, Dale R. SGT	10/9/52
Woolery, Clyde L. Jr. CPL	9/28/50
Yelton, Harold E. PFC	3/29/53

Index

page numbers in **bold** denote photographs

D

E

F

G

J

K

L

N

O

P

R

T

U

V

W

Y

57621008R00185

Made in the USA
Lexington, KY
19 November 2016